SWARTHMOOR HALL

AND ITS PEOPLE

DAVID A. JACKSON

Published in 2018 by David A. Jackson

ISBN: 978-1-9996156-9-7

Printed in the UK by INGRAM

Book & Cover Design by Russell Holden

www.pixeltweakspublications.com

A Catalogue record for this book is available from the British Library.

Printed by Ingram

Cover illustration: The 19th century view of Swarthmoor Hall

PREFACE

I joined the Swarthmoor Hall History Group, in the first instance to listen to a number of interesting lectures organised by Ian Lewis, then volunteering to sort out the family relationships of the Fells and the Abrahams both early and late and the Lindow family. Then I got interested in the date the hall was built and after that I decided I had better write a book. Partly because I was recording documents not previously published and partly because things were said about the history of both house and families without adequate evidence. In particular Margaret Askew was not related to Anne Askew the martyr, Thomas Fell was very unlikely to have been born at Hauxwell. The baptisms of George and Bridget Fell were easily discoverable being at Dalton-in-Furness. Margaret Askew later Fell finally Fox had one sister Frances and no known brothers. The Askews' claim to Marsh Grange was disputed by the Rawlinson family. Swarthmoor does not derive its name from Lambert Simnel's general Martin Schwartz. The alleged personal friendship of Judge Fell with Oliver Cromwell is unsubstantiated. However the reference in Fell's will to his great friend Lord Bradshaw is corroborated by a number of occasions when they worked together. Bradshaw presided at the trial of Charles I.

I make no attempt to enter into the mental processes of the various historical persons mentioned in the text. Many of the persons mentioned left behind very little in the way of correspondence or reported public speech. Margaret Askew Fell Fox has left a voluminous correspondence much of it reported in Maria Webb's "The Fells of Swarthmoor Hall" A great deal has been written about Margaret not least by her descendent Isabel Ross "Margaret Fell mother of Quakerism" and a great deal has been written about George Fox. Thomas Mounsey in 1845 wrote "A brief account of Thomas Fell of Swarthmoor Hall" It is concerned with the judge's spiritual life and much of it is derived from Fox's Journal. While both Margaret Fell and George Fox feature in this book they are not the chief focus. This book looks at the men of the Fell family and their servants and friends, the Lindow family and their agents and tenants. It also looks at when the Hall was built, how and when it changed hands.

Illustrations

ACKNOWLEDGEMENTS

I joined the Swarthmoor Hall History Group lead by the late Ian Lewis and have benefited by conversation with its remaining former members Margaret Bailey, Daniel Ellsworth, Neil and Vivien Hudson and Martin Riley and also from material that they had gathered. I am also indebted to the unfailing helpfulness of *The Barrow Record Office*, Susan Benson, Selina Kendall and Paul Moore, to the staff of the Parliamentary Record Office, to the archivist of University College Oxford, to the staff of the Bodleian Library Oxford, to the librarian of Brasenose College, Oxford for access to one of their rare books, to the archivist and staff of the library and archive centre at Friends House London, To the staff of the Lancashire Record Office at Preston, to Jane Pearson manager at Swarthmoor Hall, to Robert Sutton bookseller of Ulverston for tracking down various obscure publications and to Peter Lowe antiquarian book seller for many interesting and useful conversations and in particular for lending me a copy of Thomas Mounsey's book on Thomas Fell and letting me read Margaret Fell's "Relation" in Sowle's book, to Bernard and Elizabeth Ellis for much historical information about Ulverston and particularly for Elizabeth's copy of the petition regarding the Soutergate Fire, to Helen Shacklady for her book on Ulverston and encouragement and to Russell Holden for assistance with the publication of this work and to the various local history societies who have tolerated me lecturing on the subject of this book.

I should also add the invaluable help of British History online and a web site I found by typing in "Duchy of Lancaster Rentals and Surveys" and using their advanced search option. I have tried to make sure I have obtained permission to quote any copyright work extensively but sometimes it has been difficult to ascertain who if anybody owns the copyright. If I have infringed anybody's rights, I apologise and will make suitable acknowledgment in future editions.

CONTENTS

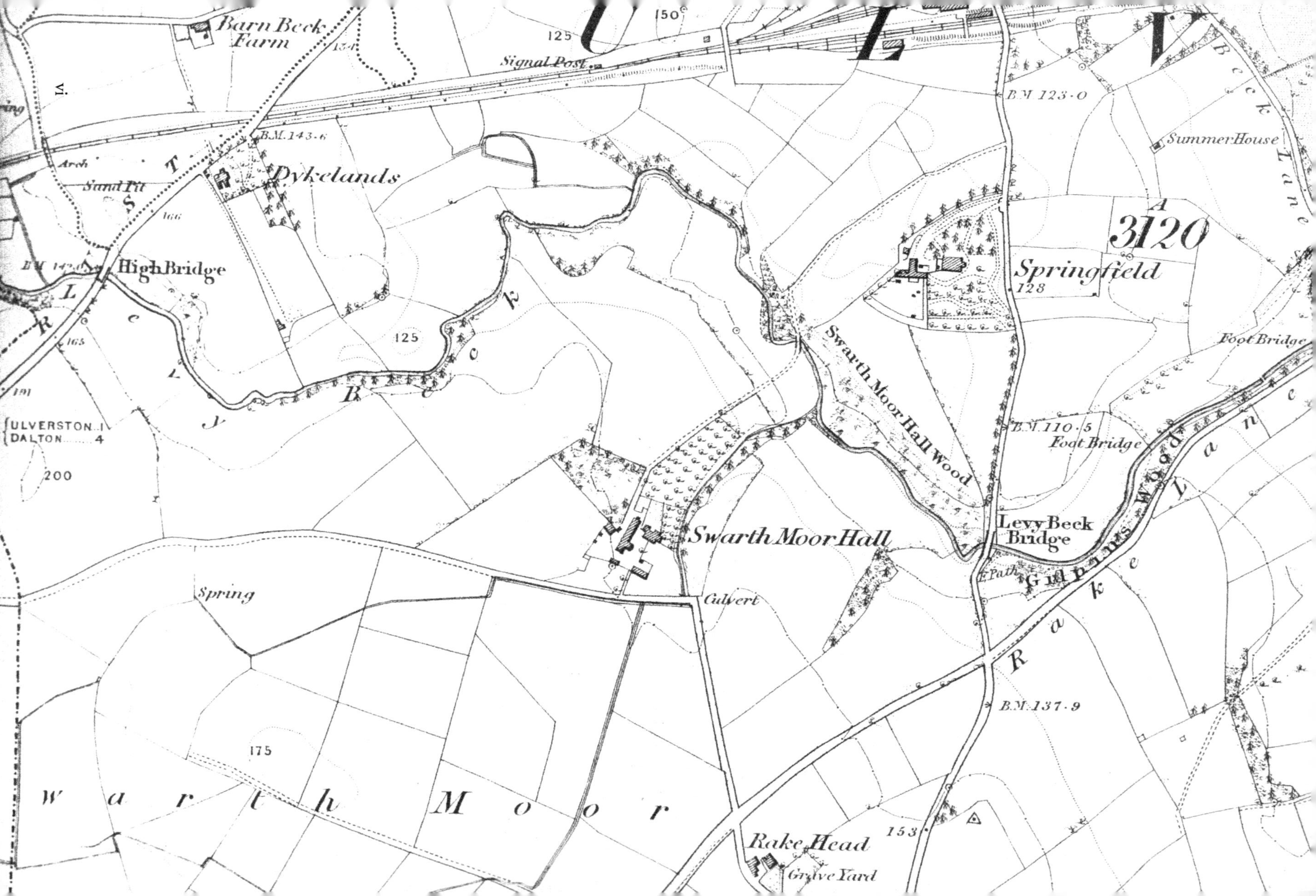

Barn Beck Farm
125
150
Signal Post
B.M. 123·0
Beck Lane
Summer House
B.M. 143·6
Dykelands
Arch
Sand Pit
166
High Bridge
3120
Springfield
128
125
Foot Bridge
Swarth Moor Hall Wood
B.M. 110·5
Foot Bridge
ULVERSTON 1
DALTON 4
200
Levy Beck Bridge
Swarth Moor Hall
Gilpins Wood
Lane
Path
Spring
Culvert
Rake Lane
B.M. 137·9
175
Swarth Moor
153
Rake Head
Grave Yard

INTRODUCTION

Swarthmoor Hall is best known for its involvement in the development of the Society of Friends better known as the Quakers. George Fox's visit in 1652 led to the conversion of the female part of the Fell family particularly that of Judge Fell's wife Margaret who later played an important roll in the life of the Quakers marrying George Fox sometime after the death of her husband. We have many letters written by or to Margaret and an account of her religious development called a "Relation of Margaret Fell" in which she tells how she came to be a Quaker. We have George Fox's journal. The "Relation" and the "Journal" give us the basic account of Fox's first visit to Swarthmoor and the conversion of much of the Fell family and their servants. We also have Sarah Fell's account book. Sarah was one of the daughters of Thomas and Margaret Fell. However less is known about Judge Thomas Fell, his father George Fell or his son George Fell, The origins of the hall itself are somewhat mysterious. The trials of the Abrahams who were descended from Rachel Fell the youngest daughter have not so far as I know been written up. Something is known about the Lindow family who followed the Abrahams as owners. More is known about the period after Emma Clerk Abraham a descendent of Rachel's acquired the property in 1912.

The first owner we know about is George Fell of Ulverston. He is followed by his son Thomas who married Margaret Askew in 1632. The first three children Margaret, Bridget and George were not born at Swarthmoor, Bridget and George were baptised at Dalton. So far as we know the other girls Isabella, Mary, Susannah, Sarah and Rachel were born at the hall. Judge Fell left the hall to his wife for her life and widowhood and no longer. It is actually more complicated than that. In 1691 Daniel Abraham who was Rachel's husband bought the hall from the rest of the family. Daniel and Rachel had one son John who followed his father and stayed at the hall till 1759. He had a son Thomas who was given the ownership of the hall but lived in Whitehaven. He went bankrupt in 1753 and eventually everything was sorted out by Thomas Petty in 1759 who then sold the hall to James Jackson brother in law and agent of William Lindow. Lindow gained actual possession of the hall in 1763. He married Abigail Rawlinson in 1772 and died in 1786 with no children. He appointed trustees and told them to give the income from the hall to Ann Jackson daughter of the previously mentioned James Jackson and his wife Ellinor; Lindow's sister. After Ann's death the hall was to go to her eldest son who was William Lindow Dickinson. He married Sarah Tompson and they had two daughters Ann and Mary. William Lindow Dickinson left all his property to his wife Sarah for her life and widowhood. His will was made 1848 and proved 1853 Ann married Henry Fletcher of Stoneleigh Workington in 1857. They had three children Amy 1858, Annie 1861 and William Lindow Fletcher 1864 who sold the hall to Miss Abraham in 1912. The Lindows were absentee landlords and it is difficult to discover who was living at the hall during there ownership

Swarthmoor is in the parish of Ulverston about a mile south of the town centre. Ulverston is a market town in the Furness Peninsula which is north of Morecambe Bay now in Cumbria but formerly in Lancashire North of the Sands. On the A590 the road from Ulverston to Barrow-in-Furness you pass through Swarthmoor village this is a nineteenth century creation to provide housing for the iron ore miners working in Lindal Moor. Swarthmoor Hall is about half a mile east of the edge of this village. The modern village is not in Ulverston but is in Pennington. Such housing as there was in Swarthmoor apart from the hall is near the Quaker Meeting House further to the east. Swarthmore in Pennsylvania is named after our Swarthmoor. There is or was another Swarthmoor near Lancaster. It is a mystery where all the people who describe themselves as of Swarthmoor actually lived. Even today the Hall is surrounded by green fields and the only accommodation for human beings was either in the Hall or in one or other of the double fronted cottages at either end of the long barn. Petty Croft where the Meeting House stands probably counted as part of Swarthmoor especially as the only subsidy roll listing Swarthmoor separately had a Petty as one of the two taxpayers. The area round Petty Croft is now almost built up with spreading suburbs of Ulverston most of which has been built since 1900 apart from a row of cottages called Petty Croft near the Meeting House. Indeed much of the housing is post war and there is no indication of housing on earlier maps. Originally Swarthmoor would be an area of rough grazing with out any housing

The English Civil War is the background to the story of the Fells. George Fell benefited from the Stuart Kings cash flow problem in that he was able to acquire the Manor of Neville Hall because King James was selling off manors, on the other hand he was fined for refusing a knighthood offered in an ingenious money making scheme of Charles I. His son was a puritan, was an officer in a parliamentary regiment, was a recruiter MP and a friend of John Bradshaw though he disagreed with him over the King's trial and execution, but the friendship and colleagueship continued. Thomas Fell did very well in the disturbed times when property was changing hands as estates were sequestrated and broken up. George Fox doesn't appear on the scene till after the King's execution. The parliamentary period gave Fox his chance and enabled him to establish the Quakers. George Fell the Judge's son was a royalist and his wife's first husband had been involved in a plot to bring Charles II to the throne much earlier than actually happened. After the Restoration things were not so comfortable for the Quakers as they had been but they benefited from the Toleration Act introduced by James VII and II for the benefit of Roman Catholics, which toleration act was reintroduced under William & Mary. Margaret Fell lived on into the reign of Queen Anne. Her son in law Thomas Lower had a brother Richard Lower who was physician to Charles II. The Abrahams were in charge under the earlier Hanoverians, the 15 and the 45 seem to have passed them by quite literally in the case of the 45 as Bonny Prince Charlie's route to Preston would presumably go through Kendall and Lancaster. When the Lindow's took over the slave trade was in full swing and the Lindows joined in though John Rous another Fell son in law had estates in the West Indies, by the time of William Lindow Dickinson the involvement of the owners of the hall with national life was over. However the money which enabled the later Abraham's to reacquire the hall was created in the commercial and industrial boom of Victorian England.

CHAPTER ONE
THE NAME SWARTHMOOR

The area is called Wart in the Domesday Book when Furness and Cartmel were part of Yorkshire. Lancashire did not come into existence until later. The name probably means Swarthy or dark moor. In the 1350s there were two hundred acres of waste in Swarthmoor and Blawith.[1] There was in the past some speculation that the name derives from that of a General Martin Schwartz who commanded the German Army assisting the invasion of Lambert Simnel in June 1487. They landed at Piel Island from Ireland. Simnel had been crown as Edward VI in Dublin. The men probably camped on Swarthmoor while the leaders stayed in Ulverston. However, the name Swarthmoor had been in use long before the invasion. In 1538 there was a dispute between the Nevilles and Thomas Stanley Lord Monteagle farmer for the crown of the former priory of Conishead concerning pasture land in Swarthmoor.[2] The Nevilles won the case. The subsidy roll for 1545 is the only one specifically mentions Swarthmoor as a hamlet or village with a list of taxpayers. There are only two one was called John Petty.[3]

In 1569 Sir John Neville joined the Rising of the North which was unsuccessful and in consequence his land was forfeit to the crown 1570. A survey of his lands which included the manor of Neville Hall was entrusted to Edmund Hall and William Homberston by a commission of 10th March 1569. This stated that Swarthmoor was in the demesne lands of Neville Hall.[4] In 4th May 1337;11 Edward III this manor had contained 30 messuages or tenements, 3 mills, 423 acres land, 30 acres meadow, 10 acres of wood, 30 acres of pasture, 10 acres of moor and 20 acres of rurbary or peat moss in Ulverston.[5] The subsidy roll of 1629 for Ulverston mentions two George Fells one of Swarthmoor and one of Ulverston. However in 1625 both these George Fells are offered knighthoods and both are described as of Warmore.[6] The first mention of Swarthmoor Hall as Swarthmoor Hall is in the sale of 1691.

CHAPTER TWO
THE FELLS

We have four male Fells father, son, grandson and great grandson George, Thomas, George and Charles. The name Fell is local and occurs already several times in the poll tax for Lonsdale 1379. By the seventeenth century there were a number of Fell families whose inter relationships are obscure if they ever existed. Fell is the local name for a hill or piece of rough ground. George Fell the elder made his will in 1638 (Appendix A) though we only have a copy dated 1681 He calls himself elder of Swarthmoor and leaves his property to his only son Thomas. He has an unmarried daughter Alice, four married daughters married to Thomas Corker, Thomas Gaitskill, Thomas Cooper and Henry Lindow. We know that Thomas Fell seems to have owned the manor of Neville Hall. Neville Hall now demolished was on the site of the former police station.

A George Fell is free tenant of Neville Hall in the Survey of 1570. He is also the only Fell mentioned.[7]

George Fell seems to have been a new man, new to wealth that is. There are Fells in the manor rolls for earlier periods but whether they are any specific connection is not certain. He was certainly wealthy. The king would not have offered him a knighthood otherwise. How he made his money is not known. He seems to have had some connection with the Fells of Scathwaite according to his grandson's will. James Fell of Scathwaite makes his will in 1606. George is not his son but may be a nephew or cousin. George Fell may be the George Fell of Ulverston mentioned as a freeholder in Lonsdale in 1600 along with Christopher Fell and Francis Corker both of Ulverston.

There is a bundle of papers in which there are a number of receipts for manorial dues relating to the manor of Neville Hall.[8] They all relate to a specific burgage plot in Soutergate in Ulverston. The first of these documents is a let in 1608 by George Fell of Marketstead Ulverston to Robert Towers In 1612 George Fell the elder of Marketstead Ulverston and his son Thomas are buying moss land

from Thomas Corker.[9] This must be the same man. In 1611 George Fell the elder of Ulverston, John Benson of Ulverston and William Kilner of Ulverston bought the manor of Neville Hall from George Salter and John Williams two Londoners who had bought it from King James I in 1609. In 1613 these three sell Waist End Ulverston to Gabriel Fell[10] and in 1618 George Fell the elder and John Benson are selling a house at Dragley Ulverston to Thomas Ashburner.[11] Further Nick Sheedy reports that in November 1607 George Fell yeoman attorney and William Kilner yeoman attorney acted as attorney for William Huddleston esquire Millom in selling Kirktarne alias Tarnclose to William Beck chapman of Kendal and widow Anne Fell by feoffment. Ann Fell's interest was to be allowed to continue living there for her widowhood and may have been a relation of George's.[11a]

I think all these George Fells are the same man and he is Thomas Fell's father. In 1623 he sends his son Thomas to Gray's Inn to train as a lawyer in their register George is described as gentleman. In 1625 comes the offer of a knighthood from King Charles I. There were disadvantages in taking a knighthood So George declined and compounded his refusal by paying a financial penalty in 1631 as did the other George Fell.[12] This was possibly why the king offered these knighthoods as the offer was made to great many gentlemen at the same time most of whom declined including John Askew of Marsh Grange, Matthew Richardson of Roanhead both of whom are involved with the Fells, William Gardiner of Bank End Urswick, John Ambrose of Lowick, Thomas Richardson of Pennington and Roger Kirby of Kirby who all compounded. There were other George Fells about at the time but before discussing them we will continue the line of the Swarthmoor Hall family.

Thomas Fell was said to be born at Hauxwell a farm on the Broughton Road from Ulverston. There is a Thomas Fell son of George baptised at Ulverston in 1599 but no place of residence mentioned. Judging by the frequency with which George Fells have their children baptised often two at different dates in the same year, we are dealing with more than one George Fell but the register does not differentiate them. However in the huge deed of 1691 when Daniel Abraham buys the hall it is stated that all four generations of Fells George, Thomas, George and Charles owned Hauxwell. When George acquired Hauxwell is not known. Certainly in earlier deeds a family called Hebson are the owners. Alexander Garnett appears in a court roll from 1594-1628 and is described as of Hauxwell from 1618 onwards. He marries Elizabeth Satterthwaite at Hawkshead in 1604 and she dies at Hauxwell in 1605/6 being buried at Ulverston. Unfortunately all that survives for Alexander's death was an inventory. However he was having children baptised at Ulverston 1611/2 - 1615. He would be a slightly younger contemporary of George Fell Snr. The most likely scenario is that George Fell purchased Hauxwell after 1629 by which time his son was at the bar. There seems to be no family connection between the Fell and Garnett families. It is unlikely that Thomas was born at Hauxwell.

Thomas may have gone to University College Oxford on the 23rd June 1621. That Thomas left 29th May 1623.[13] The Thomas at University College was among the poorer class of Undergraduates and according to the University matriculation register he was aged 19, son of a gentleman from Lancashire. He would fit nicely. He would be the right age to go to Oxford and then as a graduate go on to Gray's Inn As stated previously Thomas was admitted to Gray's Inn on 20th October 1623.[14] It was probably while he was at Gray's Inn that he met and became a friend of John Bradshaw who late presided over the trial of King Charles I. Bradshaw had gone to Gray's Inn in 1620 and was called to the bar in 1627. In 1631 Fell was called to the bar. In 1632 he had married Margaret Askew daughter of John Askew of Marsh Grange in the parish of Dalton-in-Furness. They were not married at Dalton, the marriage registers for that period have survived. It is possible that they married at the school chapel at Ireleth a precursor of the Victorian St Peters. The evidence that they did get married is that Margaret says they did in one of her letters[15]. And a deed of 3rd January 1649 refers to an earlier feoffment of 19th September 1634 made in consideration of a marriage between Thomas Fell and Margaret Askew, In 1634 Thomas Fell acquired something from John Askew.[16] The 1649 deed transfers Orgrave Mill at Dalton to Frances younger sister of Margaret Fell and wife of Matthew Richardson Jnr of Roanhead from Thomas Fell.

In 1637 he enters with John Bradshaw of Grey's Inn and William Knipe into a tenancy of land at Hoggrell's Fields Newbold Northamptonshire.[21] In 1650 Thomas Fell had bought Rouse Mill, Little Mill, Orgrave Mill and Windmill in Dalton and Cornmill, Ure Mill and Little Mill in Ulverston along with tenement called Alescale in Yarleth, a fee farm rent of £9 for land at Sandscale and the right to graze 300 milch cows on Sandes Marsh. Also in 1650 He when described as of Gray's Inn and Samuel Terricke merchant of London had purchased glebe land and tenements belonging to the rectory of Whalley and situated in Whalley, Church, Burnley, Colne, Haslingden and Clitheroe. Matthew and Frances were not married at Dalton either despite both of them being from the parish. Matthew son of Matthew Richardson of Ravenheads (presumably Roanhead) entered Gray's Inn 12th February 1637/8 and his eldest son and heir Thomas went their 4th November 1663. (This makes me wonder if the Fell Askew marriage and the Richardson Askew marriage were at Gray's Inn- However there is no surviving license for such marriages and such a license would be required - Gray's Inn Chapel registers for the period do not survive) Thomas and Margaret had two children baptised at Dalton; Bridget the second girl in 1635 when Thomas is referred to as Mr and the son George in 1638 by which time Thomas counted as esquire. As John Askew also had the use of Elliscales [17] Thomas and Margaret could have been living there or at Marsh Grange.

In 1641 Thomas Fell is Thomas Fell Esquire paying the subsidy roll as of Ulverston presumably moving to Ulverston after the death of his father in 1638. He was also in the same year appointed to the Commission for the peace for Lancashire. [18] In 1641 there was a serious fire in Soutergate destroying a number of houses and other properties, the owners of these properties seek relief and assistance and send a petition which petition is signed by many leading local residents including three separate Thomas Fells.[19] There is a lengthy gap in the Ulverston Register so there is no evidence from the Ulverston baptism register for the birth of the other five daughters or the child that died young. Margaret presumably the eldest died in London in 1706 aged 73 indicating a birth in 1633. Isabella died in 1704, Sarah in 1714 aged indicating a birth date of 1643. Mary died 1719 aged 75 indicating a birth date of 1645.[20] Susannah was alive in 1706. Rachel was dedicated in the Quaker meeting in 1653.

In 1642 Thomas became a parliamentary sequestrator of forfeitures of royalist estate for Lancashire,[21] In the Royalist Composition Papers his name appears a number of times sometimes as a member of the Lancashire Commission for Royalist Composition, sometimes as a witness to particular decisions and judgements, once as a tenant of land disputed between two royalist landlords and as being the instigator of fee farm rents for himself and others. In 1645/6 he signs the composition papers for Sir John Talbot of Salesbury. In 1646 He signs the composition papers for Revd Isaac Allen of Prestwich, In 1649 that the commission will pay certain rents in the sequestrated estate of George Middleton of Leighton. In the same year he signs the composition papers with George Dodding and others for Thomas Carus of Halton, for Walter Strickland, Again in 1649 he signs again concerning the estate of Robert Rawlinson of Marsh Grange deceased, he signs with George Dalling which may be a misreading of Dodding.. He signs the papers for

James Earl of Derby in two places, this time John Bradshaw signs as well. In 1651 he is the leading man in a contract and conveyance from the Trustees for sale of fee farm rents to himself, Thomas Birch, Gilbert Ireland, William West, John Sawrey, Robert Cundliffe and Adam Sandys to acquire fee farm rents of the Rectory of Huyton including Huyton, Roby, Woolfall, Knowsley and Tarbucck; Ormskirk, Rectory of Melling, Garstang, Rectory of Tunstall, Dalton and Ponsonby, fee farm rents for wapentages of Lonsdale and Amounderness, Pensions of Winwick and Leigh, spirituality of Altcar, tythes of Great Pulton and Little Pulton with responsibility for paying pensions of four retired clergy, schoolmasters in Middleton, Manchester and Whalley and stipends of 14 ministers of religion. In 1651 he and Thomas Birch write to the national committee recommending Evan Wall to be a member of the Lancashire commission in place of Peter Holles deceased. In 1652 He and Thomas Birch of Birch sell the manor of Haslingden to two brothers called Sharples. According to Ordinances of the Commonwealth[22] Thomas Fell was on various commissions every year from 1642 to 1654 except 1651 but plus one in 1657. He became a MP for Lancaster Borough on 6th January 1646 with Sir Robert Bindloss Bt. They replaced Thomas Fanshawe esquire and John Harrison esquire who were disabled to sit,[23] Fell withdrew from parliament rather than be involved in the trial and execution of the king before February 1649. In a letter written to Colonel John Moore a regicide MP in February 1649 the writer, Leonard Rawlinson states *"Fell has deserted the parliament and was none of those that were secluded but ran in to the country because he would not join with you that took this great work upon you {and} lurks in the country to see the event of things that so he may come in smoothly when the coast is clear"* [24] However he was readmitted to the House of Commons on July 23rd 1649 [25] having signed the declaration of dissent the day before [26] and next day appointed to the Committee for prisoners. He was reappointed to the Committee for Lancashire in December 1649 having been omitted at the reappointment in April. He is one of twenty MPs noted as having returned in November 1652 after being absent for a period.[27] In 1651 a letter from Fell then at Lancaster was received and read to the house (contents unknown). This may be when he and Thomas Birch MP for Liverpool joined the objections of the commissioner's for the peace of Lancashire to the appointment of Richard Massey a mercer from Warrington as a fourth commissioner. Fell and Birch said about Massey *"He is unable in point of experience and judgement for the implement and that he had not any estate responsible to the Commonwealth for that trust"* [28] Fell was not one of the more active or loquacious members when he was in the house. He is said to be one of the MPs who returned to the house in November 1652 after a lengthy absence Fell is referred to as an MP in a letter from, the Council of State to Col Walton in 1653. Henry Porter was elected MP for the Borough of Lancaster in 1656.[29] It was said that Cromwell gave Fell a silver cup treasured by his descendents but now lost. Also in 1646 Thomas Fell was appointed to the Presbytery of Furness [30] and was elected learned counsel at Chester in place of John Ratcliffe [31] In March 1647 parliament appointed him Attorney General for Chester and Flint relinquishing that post to John Santhey 4th February 1652/3 on becoming one of the Chief Justices of the County of Chester. He had been appointed second Judge of Chester in place of Mr Justice Warburton by the House of Commons.[32]

In 1649 he presided over a commission to enquire into the number yearly rental value and provision for maintenance and preaching ministry of all churches and chapels in the Hundred of Lonsdale. This was part of the Oliveran Survey.[33] He also held office in the Duchy of Lancaster he became both Serjeant at Law & Attorney and Serjeant 3rd August 1649 He was Vice Chancellor of the Duchy from December 1649 to May 1651 He and John Bradshaw were commissioner for the seal (effectively Chancellor) though restricted to the County Palatine. The Duchy of Lancaster had many estates outside Lancashire.[34] He became a bencher at Gray's Inn in 1651. He was associated with Bradshaw on the Northern Circuit in 1652 and on 1st January 1653 he was Chancellor alone as commissioner for pleas. He received the Duchy seal fees till July 1658. He died 8th October 1658.

He made his will in the September and it was proved in the December of that year. In addition he had been appointed to at least fifteen commissions between 1642 and 1657 mostly for raising money and mostly for Lancashire but one for the seven northern counties, one for poor prisoners and one for scandalous ministers.[35] He was said by Bulstrode Whitelock when reporting his death to have been a good judge and good lawyer [36] He was also able to purchase some Crown Lands.[37] There are reports that Judge Fell was also friendly with Cromwell but disagreed with him over the trial and execution of the king, but that Cromwell valued his presence in the house and encouraged him to return. I have to say that so far I have found no evidence of this or of the silver cup mentioned earlier. The friendship with Bradshaw is clearer principally from Fell's statement to that effect in his will but also from a number of offices they seem to have shared. George Fox in his Journal states that Judge Fell wished that he, Fox, could talk with Judge Bradshaw.

At some stage Thomas Fell had been a Lt Colonel in George Dodding's regiment on the parliamentary side. Both he and Dodding appear in a list of free burgesses of Liverpool in

1649 and he appears again in the 1651 list[38]. It is said in the church registers that he was buried in Ulverston Parish Church by torchlight under family pew which was in turn said to be under the leading edge of the gallery. However since then Ulverston Parish Church has had a number of alterations. The gallery was taken out and the floor renewed sometime in the 1880s. At that time they found under the floor a number of human bones these were taken out and buried in a tomb in the church yard close to the wall of the church. More recent alterations to provide toilets caused the demolition of this tomb and the bones were moved again to a tomb which had become empty and which had belonged to someone from Cartmel called Graves or Greaves. This is near the West End of the Church and may be the final resting place of Judge Fell and indeed others. Unfortunately Ulverston Rectory was destroyed by fire 1950-60 and many documents were lost.

Meanwhile in Judge Fell's absence George Fox the Quaker preacher had come to Ulverston and received hospitality at Swarthmoor. After hearing Fox speaking at Ulverston Parish Church Margaret Fell became convinced of the truth of Fox's message. This caused contention and hostility in the neighbourhood and Fell was met by his alarmed and alarming neighbours while crossing the Sands. On returning home he talked with Fox and while not convinced he was not alarmed by Fox's views allowed Quaker meetings to take place in the hall. Margaret and the children attended along with some of Fell's servants and presumably others. All the daughters accepted Fox as their spiritual leader but the son George did not. Judge Fell was able to protect the local Quakers from a certain amount of harassment and the meeting became established. In George Fox's preface to William Caton's autobiography Fox states that he Fox was beaten up at Ulverston and at Walney and thrust into the sea and then taken to the sessions at Lancaster where many priests appeared to testify against him. However Judge Fell and Justice West stood up for him and he was released.

Thomas Mounsey in his brief account says Fox was introduced by a friend but this is not stated in Fox's Journal. Fox tells us that the Judge allowed the use of his great hall for meeting by the Quakers. He tells us the Fell and West cross examined the witnesses after he was accused of affray at Walney giving what may be a verbatim account of Fell's examination. He tells us he arrived when Fell was absent and three weeks passed before Fell returned. He tells us that Fell had been intercepted by Lambitt the priest and Judge Sawrey but that Richard Farnworth and James Naylor were there when Fell returned and that he Fox came in and was able to convince Fell of his sincerity and Christianity. He described being attacked on the way home from Ulverston and young George Fell coming to his assistance being thrown into a beck and threatened with having all his teeth knocked out. He then goes on to describe his own trials in this attack which were considerable.

On one occasion Mary Fell aged 8 was inspired to tell the local priest Lambitt that the vials of wrath would be poured over him.

At the time of his death Thomas Fell owned Force Forge which manufactured iron. It was being worked for him by Thomas Rawlinson of Graythwaite. Shortly after Fell's death in 1658 [39] His widow Margaret with their daughter Mary bought a field at Great Biggins (near Stonebrigg Farm) in Osmotherley, which was transferred to Mary in 1668

Judge Fell's will (Appendix B) left the house and 50 acres to his wife Margaret for her life and widowhood and made all the daughters residuary legatees.. Son George was left law books. His friend Lord Bradshaw gets £10 for a mourning ring, £50 each is left for the poor of Ulverston, the poor of Dalton and for providing a schoolmaster for the children of Ulverston. The executors are Richard Ratcliffe and Thomas Carlton both yeomen though described as my menial servants, The supervisors are two known Quakers Anthony Pearson of Rampshaw in County Durham and Colonel Gervise Benson of Heaygarth in Yorkshire. However by no means all of his estate was included in his will. He owned far more than fifty acres. The supposition must be that he passed on the other property otherwise than by his will. He had inherited four water corn mills in Dalton-in-Furness.[40] He had purchased three water corn mills in Ulverston.[41] He had acquired by inheritance the manor of Neville Hall and obtained the rest of the manor of Ulverston from the Kirbys. He owned Hauxwell and many other properties listed in the tripartite indenture of 1691 (appendix E) Hauxwell and the manor of Ulverston and Blawith went to his son George. George certainly was in receipt of manorial dues and so was his widow Hannah.[42]

Cromwell died in 1658. His son Richard resigned the protectorate in 1659. The monarchy was restored General Monk welcomed Charles II to London in 1660. Monk was rewarded with a duchy and the Lordship of the manor of Furness. Soon after that Charles II began to take revenge. Cromwell and Bradshaw who had also died were dug up and "executed" Judge Fell was allowed to lie in peace but the crown proposed to sequester his estate as a grand malignant George Fell the son got a pardon in 1660 and Margaret continued to live at Swarthmoor Hall. [43] In 1664 Margaret was convicted of praemunire and imprisoned at Lancaster for four years. Her estate should have been confiscated by the Crown. However George made an appeal that the estate should be his and was granted it by the Crown.[44] Margaret was released in 1668 and married George Fox in Bristol in 1669.

By the terms of the judge's will she should have lost the house which should have then passed to the daughters and according to the Crown it now belonged to George. George did not approve of the new marriage and tried to persuade her to leave offering her an annuity of £100 [45]. In 1670 Margaret again went to jail on the accusation of the Kirbys. George was a friend of this family and his mother's friends thought George had put them up it. Before the trial and subsequent imprisonment George Fox had dictated to John Rous a letter to his new wife about this alleged intrigue in which Fox evidently believed and urged her to consult her brother in law Matthew Richardson husband of her sister Frances who was an attorney. Richardson who was not a Quaker thought George's behaviour was unseemly. On the same piece of paper Rous wrote a long letter of his own telling Margaret in detail of *"the efforts he was making to persuade George to rid himself of his prejudice against his mother's marriage, to stop plotting to have her imprisoned, and to give up his efforts to turn her and his sisters out of Swarthmore"* However Margaret Fox did go to jail and shortly after hearing this Thomas Lower husband of Mary Fell wrote a letter describing his visit to George Fell's father-in-law Edward Cook to see George but only saw George's wife Hannah who denied any intrigue on George's part but they did not believe her. [45] George died in 1670 and Margaret appealed and was released and in 1671 the Crown awarded the hall to the unmarried daughters Susannah and Rachel. [46] To complete the vexed question of the ownership of Swarthmoor Hall, Daniel Abraham (Rachel Fell's husband) bought everyone else out in 1691. It would seem that the only evidence Rous, Fox and Lower actually had, was that George was a friend of the Kirbys and General Monk; that he disapproved of his mother's marriage, that he wanted her out of the hall as he thought she had lost her right to live there. The Kirbys may well have had their own reasons for hostility towards Margaret Fox.

In 1651 during George Fell's childhood William Caton was introduced into the household to share lessons with George and to be his companion. William Caton wrote an autobiography which has been published. His origins are unknown except that Caton was kin to George's then tutor. For a time the two lads were friends sharing their life together. As well as lessons and the Quaker meeting they went out hunting, shooting and fishing like many other young men from similar backgrounds. As time went on William became more serious minded but George did not. William became a Quaker and a great admirer of the Fell family and particularly Margaret. George did not. It had been intended that William would go on to pursue his education as George was to do. William was allowed to remain at Swarthmoor as Margaret's secretary. In due course he became a Quaker preacher travelling widely and dying young. George continued to be interested in field sports and he and William drifted apart.

On 9th February 1652/3 George Fell son of Thomas Fell was admitted to Gray's Inn. On 16th July 1655 he reappears in the register of Gray's Inn. However on the 6 July 1655 he is down as being admitted a fellow commoner of Christs College

Cambridge at the age of 15 as son of Thomas Fell of Swarthmoor Hall having been to school at Little Urswick under Mr Inman. In early 1660 George was appointed a commissioner for the County of Lancaster and a commissioner for the militia.[47]

In 1660 at St Margaret Lothbury in London George married Hannah Potter the widow of Henry Potter apothecary of Blackfriars and daughter of Edward and Elizabeth Cooke. Henry Potter had been convicted of treason. He was formerly an army captain and with George Thomason was involved in Christopher Love's Plot; a conspiracy organised by Love to persuade Presbyterian gentlemen, citizens of London and minister to support the restoration of Charles II in 1651 as a covenanting monarch. Thomas Coke confessed his part and implicate others including Thomason and Potter, Love and another were executed. Cromwell persuaded parliament to pardon the rest in 1651 including Potter [48]. George's mother did not approve of this match but it went ahead. Margaret Fell had not approved of Margaret's marriage to John Rous, Mary's marriage to Thomas Lower and Rachel's married to Daniel Abraham but they had all taken place. Hannah's sister Elizabeth had married Richard Tomlinson also an apothecary of Covent Garden. He had translated Jean de Renou's "*Medical Dispensatory*" sometimes known as "*Renodeus*". In his 1675 PCC will he makes Hannah guardian of his children if his wife did not live long enough.

George and Hannah had the following children: Thomas in 1666 baptised and buried at Ulverston, Sarah born in London and buried at Dalton 1669, Hannah baptised and buried 1667, Isabella baptised at Dalton in 1668 and Charles baptised at Dalton 1669/70. George died in 1670 leaving his widow Hannah with two very young children. In his will (Appendix C) He wants to be buried in Ulverston as near to his father as possible. Father was buried under the family pew. All the property goes to son Charles with provision for daughter Isabel to get the income from mills in Furness. If both children die young the next heir is Thomas Fell of Scathwaite (presumably a relative) and failing him Edward Fell of Stopyard (sic) in Cheshire. He leaves various mills in Dalton and Ulverston and the manors of Ulverston, Swarthmore and Osmotherley with land about Dragley Beck. He appoints Edward Cooke and Sackville Greaves as tutors for his children. In the event both Charles and Isabel grow up and have children. In August 1670 by deed poll he had transferred Marsh Grange to Sackville Greaves to pay his debts and make provision for his infant daughter Isabel.[49] Greaves sold Marsh Grange a few months after George's death to Sarah Fell. Apparently despite this Hannah and her children continued to live there for a time.

In 1676 Sarah Fell sold Marsh Grange to Thomas Lower who lived there. Hannah had presumably moved by then. When Isabel grew up she married James Greaves and moved to Sussex. Nobody seems to have disputed George's right to own or dispose of Marsh Grange. It has to be said that virtually every piece of writing relating to George is hostile to him. In his appeal to the king in 1664 he did describe Quakerism as a fanatical opinion but he may have simply been quoting the charge against her.

However before continuing the story with Hannah's widowhood I ought to catch up with the rest of the family.

In 1661 Margaret Fell Jnr married John Rous, In 1662 Bridget Fell married John Draper of Headlam in Durham. In 1664 Isabel Fell marries William Yeomans He died in 1674 and Isabel remarried Abraham Morrice. Mary married Thomas Lower in 1668 at Swarthmoor, Thomas Lower was the brother of Richard Lower also a doctor who became physician to Charles II. Sarah married in 1681 William Mead a London merchant, Rachel married in 1682/3 Daniel Abraham and in 1691 Susanna married William Ingram. In 1683 Rachel her husband and Margaret Fox were sent to jail being prosecuted and tried by the Kirbys. However in 1686 a royal warrant and general pardon of James II lead to them being released from prison

In the same bundle of documents in which George Fell sells a lease on land in Soutergate to Robert Towers is a receipt from Hannah Fell for twelve pence from William Towers for the same land as manorial dues on the death of the lord of the manor George Fell, Hannah as guardian acting on behalf of the new lord Charles Fell who was an infant. Apparently the Fell sisters and their mother Margaret continued to call on Hannah and Charles at Marsh Grange.

In 1678 the Fell sisters with John Rous and Thomas Lower conveyed the manor of Osmotherley to Charles Fell (despite it being in his father's will) It is possible

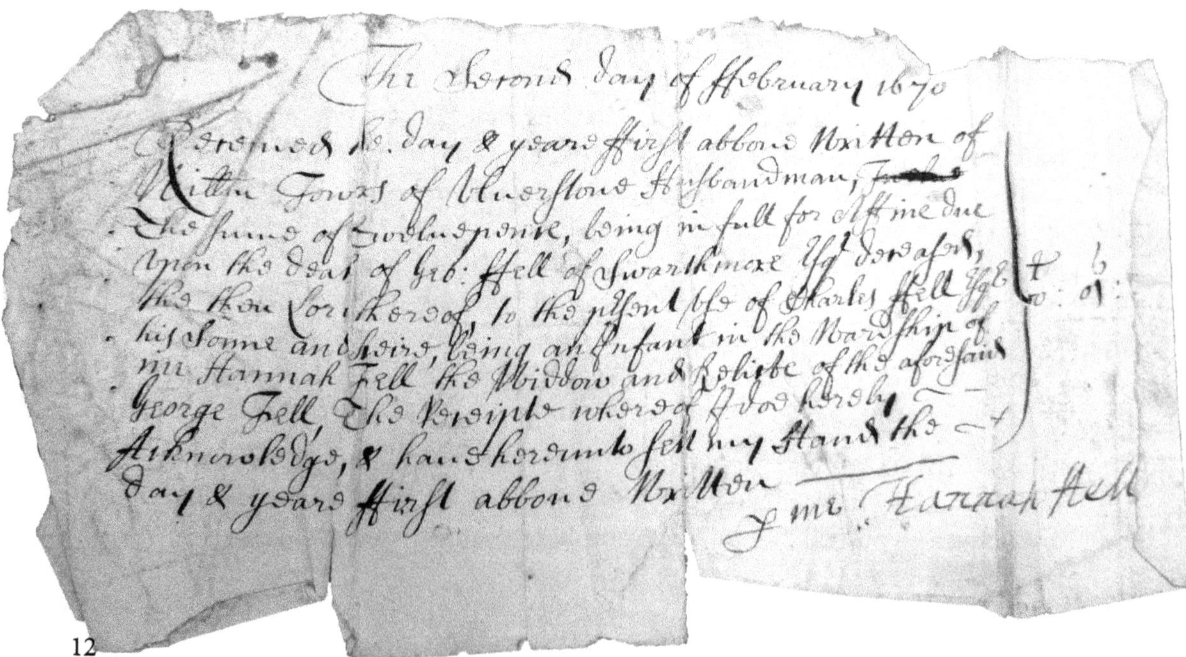
The Seconde day of ffebruary 1670
Receved the day & yeare ffirst abbove written of
William Towers of Ulverstone Husbandman,
the summe of twelvepence, being in full for a ffine due
upon the death of Geo: ffell of Swarthmore Esq deceased,
the then Lord thereof, to the present use of Charles ffell Esq
his Sonne and heire, being an Infant in the Wardship of
mr Hannah Fell the Widdow and Relicte of the aforesaid
George Fell, The Receipt whereof I doe hereby
Acknowledge, & have hereunto sett my Hand the
day & yeare ffirst abbove written
p me Hannah Fell

that at this stage Hannah and Charles were living in a house in Ulverston which was later referred to in the indenture tripartite of 1691. In 1687 Hannah returns to the attack by closing the footpath from Ulverston to the hall. This is presumably the present path starting from Springfield Road and traversing Longdales passing between Kilner Park Estate and the Roman Catholic School descending a steep bank crossing a small stone bridge and ascending the field to the hall. The bridge is too narrow for any sort of wheeled traffic bigger than a small cart though probably negotiable on horseback. So it is not the only means of access but by far the most convenient for pedestrians. In some cases a lord of the manor has or had the right to close paths across manorial land or charge for their use. It is still causing trouble in various places today. If she had no possible legal powers why did the hall servants not simply remove the obstacle. On another occasion she had the gate between the hall and the path locked. There has been discussion on why she did this but none on how and with what right..

In 1688 George Fox gave the land and buildings at Petty Croft for a meeting house for the Quakers. He had previously purchased this land from Susannah and Rachel Fell.

In 1691 George Fox died and Charles Fell came of age. Charles Fell seems to be based in London which may have made him willing to sell out and Daniel Abraham was willing to buy. The indenture tripartite (Appendix E) of 1691 is a lengthy document in which Daniel buys out not only Charles and Hannah but Isabell and all his sisters in law with their spouses, even paying his wife something. It lists all the properties currently in the hands of various Fells except Marsh Grange which was owned by Thomas Lower. It describes the location of house which Hannah had lived in King St Ulverston It states that Hauxwell had belonged to all four Fells from George Sr to Charles, It mentions manors and watermills and numerous properties in Ulverston including the apothecary's which is still used for the same purpose. It mentions land and property in many parts of Low Furness. Signatures of all the interested parties were attached including Margaret Fox, Charles Fell, Hannah Fell all the daughters and their husbands, Charles's sister and husband and the surviving executor of Judge Fell's will. Two intermediaries were used Thomas Richardson of Roanhead esquire with John Corker of Lund in Ulverston gentleman as parties of the second part and Richard Rawlinson gentleman Ulverston and Thomas Richardson of Whinfield in Furness gentleman as parties of the third part The first Thomas Richardson might well be the Thomas Richardson second son of Matthew Richardson Junior and Frances Askew. Margaret Fox died in 1701 and in her will (Appendix D) she left her property to her daughter Rachel. Also in 1691

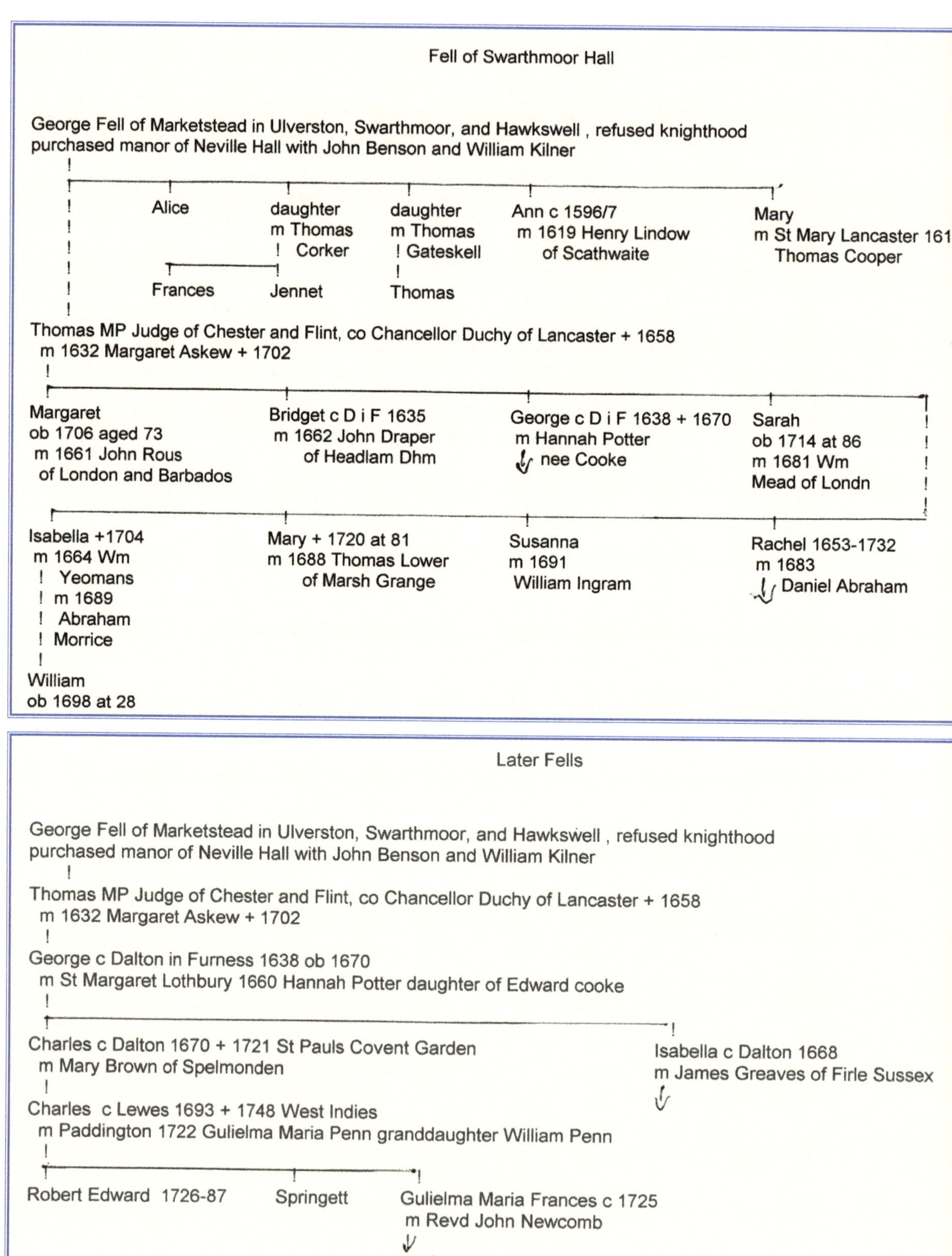
Fell of Swarthmoor Hall
George Fell of Marketstead in Ulverston, Swarthmoor, and Hawkswell , refused knighthood
purchased manor of Neville Hall with John Benson and William Kilner
Alice
daughter
m Thomas
Corker
daughter
m Thomas
Gateskell
Ann c 1596/7
m 1619 Henry Lindow
of Scathwaite
Mary
m St Mary Lancaster 161
Thomas Cooper
Frances
Jennet
Thomas
Thomas MP Judge of Chester and Flint, co Chancellor Duchy of Lancaster + 1658
m 1632 Margaret Askew + 1702
Margaret
ob 1706 aged 73
m 1661 John Rous
of London and Barbados
Bridget c D i F 1635
m 1662 John Draper
of Headlam Dhm
George c D i F 1638 + 1670
m Hannah Potter
nee Cooke
Sarah
ob 1714 at 86
m 1681 Wm
Mead of Londn
Isabella +1704
m 1664 Wm
Yeomans
m 1689
Abraham
Morrice
Mary + 1720 at 81
m 1688 Thomas Lower
of Marsh Grange
Susanna
m 1691
William Ingram
Rachel 1653-1732
m 1683
Daniel Abraham
William
ob 1698 at 28
Later Fells
George Fell of Marketstead in Ulverston, Swarthmoor, and Hawkswell , refused knighthood
purchased manor of Neville Hall with John Benson and William Kilner
Thomas MP Judge of Chester and Flint, co Chancellor Duchy of Lancaster + 1658
m 1632 Margaret Askew + 1702
George c Dalton in Furness 1638 ob 1670
m St Margaret Lothbury 1660 Hannah Potter daughter of Edward cooke
Charles c Dalton 1670 + 1721 St Pauls Covent Garden
m Mary Brown of Spelmonden
Isabella c Dalton 1668
m James Greaves of Firle Sussex
Charles c Lewes 1693 + 1748 West Indies
m Paddington 1722 Gulielma Maria Penn granddaughter William Penn
Robert Edward 1726-87
Springett
Gulielma Maria Frances c 1725
m Revd John Newcomb
modern descendants

Mary Fell's husband Dr Thomas Lower had bought three water mills and a wind mill in Dalton-in-Furness from Charles Fell. [50] One of the witnesses was Edward Cooke presumably Hannah Fell's brother

The sale to Daniel Abraham resolved the family dispute Charles Fell moved South married Mary Brown from Spelmonden in Kent had a son Charles. The elder Charles died in 1723. In the same year at St James Paddington the younger Charles married Gulielma Maria granddaughter of William Penn the Quaker founder of Pennsylvania. The Penn family owned a considerable amount of land in Pennsylvania. The younger Charles died in 1748 in the West Indies. He had two sons Lt Col Robert Edward Fell 1726-1787 and Springett Fell both died without issue. He also had two daughters one of whom Gulielma Maria married John Newcomb the Vicar of Leir in Leicestershire. There are descendants of this marriage to the present day

Thomas Lower continued to live at Marsh Grange. He died in 1720 He and Mary had many children four of whom lived long enough to marry. There was at least one descendent in recent times in 1928 and there may well be others.

There are great difficulties in sorting out what actually happened in the various disputes in that virtually all the sources are from supporters of Margaret Fell Fox. However some of the letters and speeches quoted from these people in Maria Webb and Isabel Ross are decidedly intemperate by modern standards and one quite imagine them causing considerable indignation and resentment on the other side. The imprisonment of Margaret Fox, Daniel and Rachel Abraham in 1683 after trial by two Kirbys shows that the Kirbys needed no encouragement from George Fell to act against Margaret Fox. Also George died in 1670. How long was he ill? If he was being harangued by his relatives while he was dying his widow might well have felt the Fell family were her enemy. In the Furness Compert Book for 1683 Hannah is listed as not paying for the upkeep of the parish church. She is referred to as Dame Hannah Fell a further indication of her status as acting lady of the manor.

EXCURSUS I

THE DATE THE HALL WAS BUILT

Looking at the websites and existing literature various dates are proposed for the hall being built but without supporting evidence. There is no account of its building in contemporary sources that I have yet come across. It is widely thought to be Elizabethan I disagree. I think the hall at its present size is Cromwellian. There may well be a smaller building incorporated in the present building but that was extended. If we look at the taxation records there is noticeable change between 1641 and 1660. The earlier taxation was the subsidy rolls which are records of taxation paid by individuals for special purposes of the king usually involving paying for war. There were two types one was based on the land and property owned by the individual and took the total potential income from land and buildings as its starting point. The other was based on the individuals goods, not counting crops still in the field but counting them once harvested. The figure was based on the capital value of these gifts. The crown charged the subsidy on the higher of the two figures. The records are by county and hundreds. Our hundred is Lonsdale. In some years only the total for each settlement is noted in others the amount paid by individuals is set down. It is this latter group that are of interest. In no case are the Fells paying anything out of the ordinary via the subsidy roll whereas other people were. The last subsidy roll is 1641.

The various years are set out below,. Most records are at *The National Archives at Kew* 1629 is in Cumbria Archives at Barrow-in-Furness.

1621
The assessors are William Corker, Christopher Fell, Edward Geldart & John Tennant The standard payment is £.3.40

George Fell pays £.3.40 on lands. George Fell junior pays £3.40 on goods

1624 ie 21 James I
The two George Fells both pay £3.80 as do John Lindoe, Edward Geldart, William Singleton, John Twisaday, Robert Scales, Robert Singleton, Thomas Benson and Francis Corker

William Corker of Neville Hall pays £10, Miles Phillipson and Miles Dodding both pay £10/16/- for Conishead

1626 ie 1 Charles I
Anthony Sawrey is paying £10/8/- for Plumpton, Miles Phillipson, Mrs Bridget Basbell and William Corker are paying the same. Miles Dodding esquire is paying £4/16/-. The two George Fells are paying the standard rate. The one paying of goods is of Ulverston. New to the list are Richard Fell and Henry Lindowe of Dragley Beck.

1641 *Ulverston township*
One George Fell has gone, the other is of Swarthmoor. Thomas Fell esquire has no particular place name. Richard Fell is at Mountbarrow, John Benson at Mansriggs and Henry Lindowe at Dragley Beck. All Fells are paying the standard amount.

The Hearth Tax commences after the restoration and as its name implies is based on the number of hearths

1663
George Fell and his mother are paying £8-3-4 in terris exactly the same as Miles Dodding and his mother

1664
Mrs Margaret Fell is paying for 10 hearths

1671
George Fell is paying for 13 hearths

The clear implication is that Swarthmoor Hall got a lot bigger between 1641 and 1663. Added to this there is a date stone inside the hall (not in its original position) which states *"TF 1651 JA 1716"*. George Fox arrived in 1652 to find a household of man and wife and seven children three or four resident servants and able and willing to put him up. Further in 1641, Thomas Fell esquire was not apparently living in Swarthmoor but elsewhere in Ulverston. He may have started work on the hall. JA; John Abraham his grandson obviously thought his grandfather completed some building work in 1651. On entering the hall there is a step down to passage level and to enter the room on the left you have to step up again but not with the room on the right. When the extension work was done it is possible the passage was lowered to giver a higher and more impressive ceiling. So the hall as it now stands is Cromwellian. The stile is Tudor/Jacobean but rather plain and is therefore fifty years out of date. I gather this is by no means impossible

Unfortunately the extensive local taxation of the parliamentary period has not left any records naming taxpayers or how much they paid. I gather Charles II refused to regard Parliament as a proper authority, dating his reign from his father's death and had ordered the destruction of all such local taxation records as part of his attempt to wipe out the Interregnum. Consequently we do not know what tax Thomas Fell paid during that period or what his tax was based on or the tax of any one else either.

It has been suggested that it was much bigger with an extra wing. I can find no evidence of this. Thomas Scattergood in the 1790s found the garden in a ruinous conditioned and the house dilapidated. [51] S.Lewis in his Topographical Dictionary of England published 1848 says Swarthmoor Hall was dilapidated. He also said George Fox's bed was there and visitors were allowed to sleep in it, so the hall was habitable. [52] Maria Webb regarded the house as dilapidated in the 1860s. Canon Ayre was shown round in about 1900. [53] Emma Clark Abraham did some exten-

sion work at the rear in her time. Her architect recommended clearing some very dilapidated parts of the structure on the North East corner his work uses this space to build some rooms which are now used for accommodation for visitors. [54] Young William Fell a schoolboy talks of the deplorable condition of the building and may have said some had fallen down.

In 1829 Alfred Burgess made an etching allegedly showing the hall in the seventeenth century. There are two figures in the foreground apparently dressed as puritans of the 1650s and 1660s. The interesting thing is the Burgess depicts the hall with only part of it reaching three stories the Eastern end being only two stories. If Burgess is correct at some stage the building was increased in size but whether by the Abrahams or the Lindows is difficult to tell. [55] Apart from that the only evidence of anything either falling down or being taken down is the demolition of the long barn which was taken down by the Society of Friends. They now have various meeting rooms and accommodation for visitors on approximately the same site. As this barn goes back to 1741 [56] at the latest and had at one stage double fronted houses at either end this is rather a pity. Hindsight is a wonderful thing. One possibility is that the inhabited house at Swarthmoor which preceded the present hall was not a smaller building on the same site but one of these houses. There are a number of drawings of the house from various times from which one thing is clear. On the earlier drawings the end of the hall nearest the barn was only two stories whereas the rest was three. At some stage a third story was added to this end and this was before Emma Clark Abraham bought the Hall. It seems likely that this upwards extension of the end adjacent to the barn was put in hand while the Lindows owned the building.

EXCURSUS II
THE OTHER FELLS

There is a George Fell a tailor of Swarthmoor making his will in 1665.

He has a wife Elizabeth and five children Thomas, Elizabeth, George, Edward and John and a brother Brian a cordwainer in Manchester. He leaves a messuage in Swarthmoor and a field called Cocker's Close near Mountbarrow

There is a John son of George Fell senior of Swarthmoor baptised at Ulverston in 1654 and a Brian son of George in 1598 either or both may tie in with this will.[57]

There is also George x Fell yeoman the eldest of Swarthmoor whose will was made 1655 and proved 1660 He may be the other George Fell of Swartmoor who was offered a knighthood. He had several wives. He refers to a wife Margaret but asks to be buried near his late wives. He had an eldest son Edmund already deceased who had five daughters Ann, Elizabeth, Ruth Margaret and Elin. He has a son Miles who has a son Thomas. He has a daughter Margaret wife of William Simpson who possibly was previously married to a Geldart. His father-in-law is Robert Gardnett

The supervisors are John Sawrey of Plumpton and John Fell of Row End.

There is a Myles son of George baptised at Ulverston in 1607 but that George was a dyer in Ulverston

There is also Mary Fell widow of Swarthmoor Hall left her will in 1708 which was proved 1709. She is probably the widow of Leonard Fell one of Judge Fell's servants who became a Quaker preacher.. She left the residue of her estate to Daniel Abraham and claimed Rachel Abraham as a friend. I think she was formerly Mary Askew and may well be the servant of that name known to have been at the hall in Judge Fell's time.

She had a nephew Anthony Askew a whitesmith in Lancaster, presumably another nephew James Askew plumber of Lancaster already deceased with children Christopher and Katherine, another deceased nephew James Askew of Sikehouse Broughton-in-Furness with children James, Esther and Ellen, nieces Elizabeth and Bridget Askew. Another niece Mary was married to James Lenteth of Millom. They had six daughters.

Also mentioned is John Fell whitesmith of Ulverston a minor beneficiary and son of another John Fell whitesmith who died in 1687. He married Sarah Benson of the Mansriggs family and they had many children including Abraham who was a Quaker and Stephen who was a Quaker and a doctor. This Stephen bought the apothecary's shop from John Abraham in 1737 58 and died in 1777.

His son was Dr John Fell who was the Quaker doctor who brought Sir John Barrow into the world and also had William Thornton as an apprentice apothecary 1777-1781. Thornton later qualified as a doctor and after moving to the United States entered the competition to design the Capitol Building for Washington and won. The present building is largely his.

It is possible that John Fell whitesmith is kin to Mary's deceased husband. In 1737 the next plot to Stephen Fell's apothecary was owned by James Fell innkeeper who built a new house.[59] There is on the building a hopper head dated 1736. The building is now Eric Ward's hairdressing establishment and a representative of the historic Buildings Commission reported that the building was basically Jacobean.

James and Stephen had a dispute about boundaries which was adjudicated on by Myles Sandys Esquire of Graythwaite Hall, John Benson gentleman of Mansriggs & Thomas Townson yeoman of Pennington. Benson was a relative of Stephen Fell.

James Fell sold the building to George Fell a butcher. James made his will in 1742 and his heir was his son John Fell of Grays Inn London who sold land at West End in 1743 to George Brockenbank. This John Fell is at Gray's Inn 11th October 1749. James had bought the land at West End in 1728 from Gabriel Fell of Seacomb in County Durham.

James Fell had three other sons George, Miles and William and two daughters Margaret & Eleanor. George Fell butcher left his will in 1758 as well as the shop in Ulverston Market Place and a nearby stable, barn and slaughterhouse. He had land near Dragley Beck and mossland near Oubas Hill. He refers to the will of his father James, his wife Ann and sister Ellen married to Samuel Killner mariner and sister Margaret married to Isaac Rawlinson. George and Ann apparently had no children. It would seem that George Fell the butcher was the son of James. It has been said that James and Stephen were brothers. This is possible, Stephen did have a brother James who was twenty two years older than him. Stephen was born to a Quaker family in 1702 to John and Sarah Fell, his father being a whitesmith. He had an elder brother also Stephen who had presumably died. He married a Quaker and his son was a Quaker. His elder brother James was born 1678. However James Fell the innkeeper's son John went to Grays Inn to train for the law. He would not have been admitted as a Quaker.

There is another Fell family with land in Swarthmoor but who didn't live there We start with three Fell brothers John, William and Richard, John is of Rowride and leaves a will in 1577, Richard is of Trinkeld. John has several sons Thomas who has a son John, Richard and Bryan. John also has daughters one married to Leonard Fell, another married to Thomas Fell of Whinnersyke. Richard of Trinkeld has a son Richard, also of Trinkeld. This Richard has land at Swarthmoor which in 1612 he leaves to his son John who leaves it his brother Christopher in 1615. John and Christopher have two other brothers Richard of Barnbeck and George and a sister married to John Fell of Raw. Richard of Trinkeld will 1612 has a grandson Richard.

A John Fell of Raw who is not necessarily the same man the one above also has a wife Margaret who leaves a will in 1612. They have four sons George, James of Channonhouse, William and Gabriel. With a daughter Agnes married to Henry Fell and a daughter Jenet married to William Fell of Holebiggerah. The matter is further complicated because the family of Fell of Dalton Gate and of Flan also start off with ancestors at Trinkeld and Rowend [60] With further complication in that Andrew Fell of Dalton Gate and his son John both leave money to John Fell the whitesmith or his children.

George Fell junior of Swarthmoor Hall made provision for the estate if his children died young. The first choice was Thomas Fell of Scathwaite.

Thomas had five children baptised at Ulverston:- Thomas 1672 Sarah1675, John 1676, Jane 1688 and Hannah 1690. An earlier Thomas Fell of Scathwaite had a daughter Jane who married John Lindow of Newland in 1653. He is possibly either the Thomas Fell of Scartherwhit appointed to the Classis for Furness in the Presbytery of Lancaster along with Thomas Fell Esquire (Judge Fell) in 1646 or his son. I think this the best clue to the origin of the Fell family of Swarthmoor Hall

His second choice was Edward Fell of Stopyard in Cheshire. Stopyard has been transcribed Stockport by some. Edward Fell of Stockport took the sacrament of the Lords Supper at Manchester Parish Church on Sunday 4th October 1674 as certified by the minister, churchwarden and two others.[61]

EXCURSUS III [62]

THE SERVANTS

Thomas Salthouse who was Judge Fell's agent. He was one of four brothers from Dragley Beck. He became a Quaker. A number of Salthouses were prominent in the life of the Meeting House. For example Joseph Salthouse, Elijah Salthouse Thomas Salthouse together with William Woodburn, William Benson and Joseph Goad acting as trustees for the Quaker meeting house are assigned a parcel of ground on Swarthmoor in the Enclosure Act 1813.[63] In 1845 John Abraham of Liverpool visited the hall when a widowed Mrs Salthouse was the tenant.[64]

Leonard Fell son of Thomas Fell of Baycliffe. He became a prisoner for his beliefs. He was in jail at Lancaster for two months in 1683 He married twice but had no children. He married his first wife Agnes Chambers in 1653. She died in 1662. (DNB) His second wife was called Mary. She died in 1708. He died in Darlington in 1701. His widow Mary administers his estate along with John Fell of the parish of Ulverston and Joseph Wood of Baycliffe. James Fell a Quaker from Hutton was also involved in the administration. Leonard Fell's brother Thomas married in 1678 at James Fell's house at Wellhouse Mary Goad of Baycliffe and from this couple a family of Fell of Warrington descend. If Leonard's widow Mary was in fact his former fellow servant Mary Askew then the John Fell of Ulverston who co administers the estate would likely be John Fell whitesmith who was a Quaker.

Henry Fell was a member of the household, though in what capacity we do not know He was an early convert and also became a preacher and worked in the West Indies. He attempted to go to India to meet Prester John but was turned back at Alexandria. As he set out for Barbados from Bristol he makes some provision for his estate in England including sums of money either given to or already in the hands of various people, including Margaret Fell, Leonard Fell, young Mr Fell and Henry's brother Thomas. He was married between 1662 and 1666. He was last heard of in Barbados

William Caton who has already been mentioned. He was brought to Swarthmoor by his father as a companion for George Fell Jr and later accompanied him to School.; Earlier he and George had shared a tutor who was kin to Caton and a priest (possibly Thomas Lawson of Rampside). He too became a travelling preacher. He was married and wrote his autobiography largely concerning his spiritual life and his travels as a preacher. [65]

Mary Askew a devoted servant mentioned by Judge Fell in his will. She may possibly be the Mary Fell of Swarthmoor Hall whose will is noted above. In which case it is more likely she is a Broughton-in-Furness Askew rather than a Marsh Grange Askew.

Ann Clayton who later joined the community of Friends in Barbados and was the wife of two successive Quaker governors of Rhode Island. Richard Clayton a member of the Swarthmoor Meeting and possibly her brother became a travelling preacher working in Cornwall and Northern Ireland.

EXCURSUS IV

MARGARET FELL'S BACKGROUND

Margaret was definitely the daughter of John Askew of Marsh Grange. She had one sister Frances[66] who married Matthew Richardson Jnr of Roanhead in Dalton. Frances developed some sort of mental illness as testified by Sarah Fell in a document where she agreed to Thomas Jon of Marsh Grange administering the goods of her uncle Matthew Richardson.[67] As Matthew Richardson and Thomas Fell acquired all the known property of John Askew at Marsh Grange and in Dalton it would seem likely Margaret and Frances had no surviving brothers. Margaret was married in 1632 at the age of nineteen according to her own testimony. She also seems to imply that the Askews had had gentry status for a long time. Her father had a nephew William Spenceley of Dalton who on one occasion acted as his proctor. William was the son of Bartholemew Spenceley by his wife Janet Askew. He was baptised at Dalton-in-Furness 1614. His parents had married their 1607.[68]

There were certainly Askews at Marsh Grange before Margaret's father. Richard Askew of Marsh Grange left a will in 1551 leaving a wife Janet and three sons William, John and Roger.[69] Of these sons John died without issue and William sold a moiety of Marsh Grange 1580 to Leonard Rawlinson of Broughton Tower, William's mother Janet being alive at the time and according to the said Leonard Rawlinson William sold him the other moiety in 1581. This is his pleading in 1586.[70] Roger however claimed that under his father's will Jenet was to have the estate for ten years if she did not remarry and after that to be divided between his two eldest sons. As John had died he; Roger was under his father's will entitled to John's moiety. Rawlinson replied that as the property was under customary tenure in the Manor of Furness, Richard was not entitled to leave the tenancy to anyone other than his proper heir which was his eldest son. Roger left a will in 1593 with a son Richard. This Richard may be the Richard Askew of Marsh Grange who left a will in 1657. He calls his widow Agnes but the issue is confused by Ann Askew widow of Marsh Grange who makes a will in 1674. Ann is presumably Richard's widow as they have the same grandchildren. Richard has sons William, Thomas and John and three daughters Richard is probably a slightly older contemporary of Judge Fells which makes it possible that his son John is Judge Fells father-in-law but not certain. Brownbill seems to think the John Askew's father was called William though where he gets this information from I do not know.[71]

In 1648 writing to the Colonel John Moore of the Committee for the advance of Moneys Leonard Rawlinson,[72] grandson of the above mentioned Leonard Rawlinson also made a claim to Marsh Grange claiming that his Uncle Robert Rawlinson of whom he is the heir mortgaged Marsh Grange to John Preston for £100. Leonard is willing to pay this £100 and regain the land. Further his father John Rawlinson had a debt of £150 borrowed from Robert Rawlinson. John's executrix is his widow Elizabeth Leonard's mother. The bonds to both debts are in the hands of Margaret widow of Robert Rawlinson now married to John Kirkby Robert Rawlinson's executer. Robert Rawlinson and John Preston are both described as delinquents presumably then royalists as is Leonard's mother Elizabeth. Leonard is a parliamentarian and his mother persuaded the cavaliers to sack his house.

In 1649 Leonard Rawlinson states that he still has not retrieved Marsh Grange saying that *"Fell has devised a scheme to keep him (Rawlinson) out of it. Mr Pym's children have an ordinance for certain sums out of Preston's estate and the trustees have given a lease of Marsh Grange to that old knave John Askew on account of a debt of £100 borrowed of old Mr Preston on that security".* A reply tells him *"It was not Preston's money but his lands that were granted to Pym's children and a word from Rawlinson and Pym would order them not to meddle with Marsh Grange Fell who aims at it was not one of those that helped in this great work, but lurks in the country to see the event of things, that so he may come in smoothly when the coast is clear' and that Askew his father-in-law has been in arms against parliament. Discover his estate and I will find you proofs to sequester it."* Rawlinson in reply states that Askew is the father of one of the trustees of Mr Pyms children, Presumably father-in-law is meant as Askew only had two daughters. However the judgement is that Askew is allowed to harvest his crop and then hand over to the Rawlinsons.

The Mr Pym would be John Pym MP one of the five members arrested by Charles I but he died in 1643 so the person referred to as being willing to keep off Marsh Grange would be one of his sons possibly Charles who was also an MP, though ejected in Pride's Purge. Colonel Moore was a regicide.

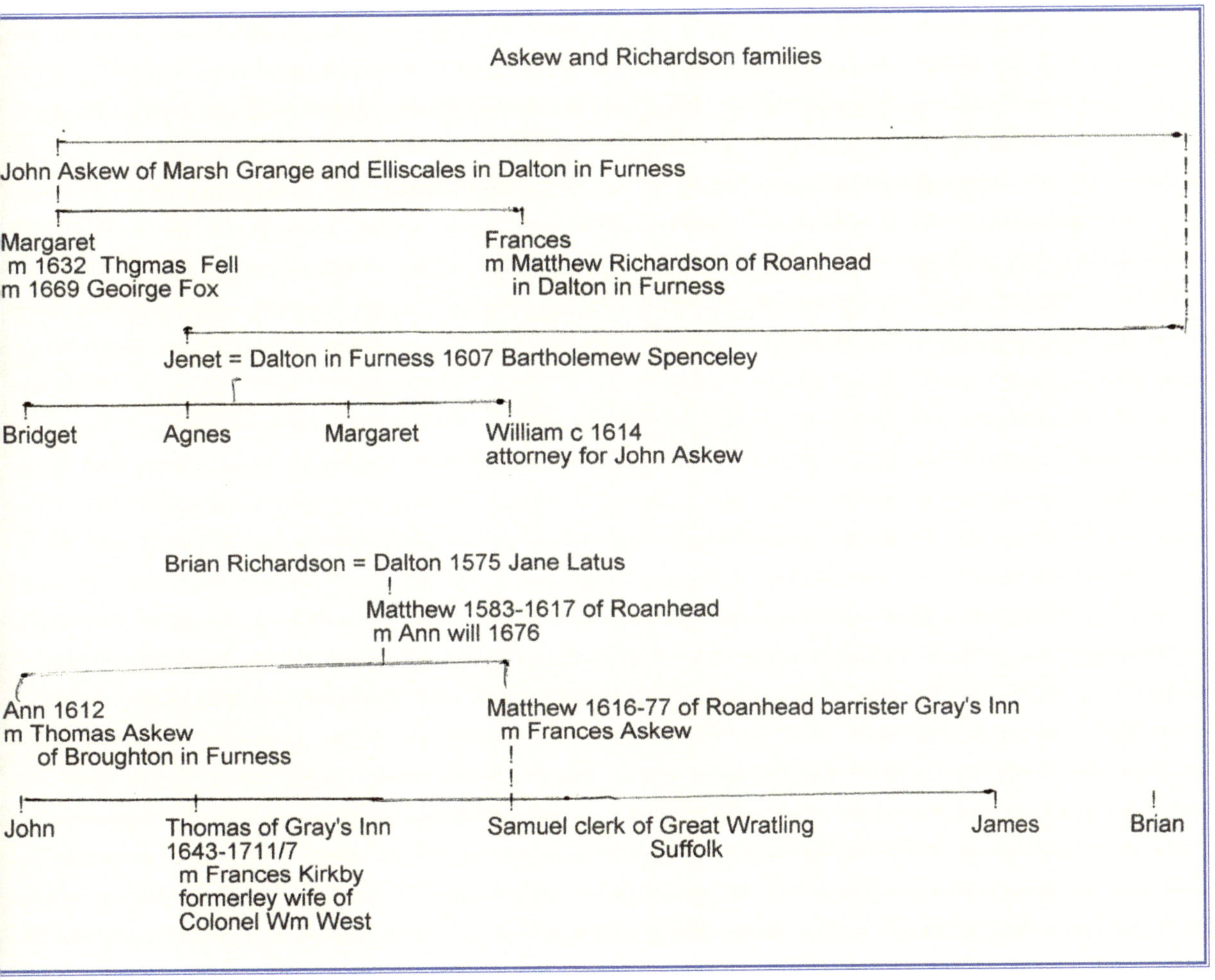

EXCURSUS V

OTHER SWARTHMOOR RESIDENTS BEFORE 1691

Ellen Barrett of Swarthmoor has an Anglican license to marry John Fell of West End and has a Thomas Fell as bondsman in 1666

Thomas Collinson yeoman Swarthmoor acts as a bondsman for Christopher Fell of Ulverston to get a license to marry 1668/9

Samuel Greaves of Swarthmoor has a license to marry 1686 A Thomas Greaves of Swarthmoor is his bondsman. This Thomas Greaves makes his will 1691 of Swarthmoor

William Fell yeoman Swarthmoor has a license to marry 1689 his bond is another William Fell of Swarthmoor yeoman.

CHAPTER THREE
THE ABRAHAMS

Richard Abraham was a grocer in Warrington dying in 1659.[73] He had a number of children including John baptised 1629 the second child of that name an earlier one having been baptised and buried 1623. John moved to Manchester and became a merchant marrying Rachel Owens of Manchester. He lived at Etchells near Stockport till his death in 1681 and was buried in the Friends burial ground in Deansgate. He was a very successful merchant and an early member of the Quakers. He had two daughters Margaret who married Edward Cheetham a great nephew of the celebrated Humphrey Cheetham, the other married Phineas Pemberton and with him emigrated to America. Pemberton became speaker of the house of assembly for Pennsylvania.

John's only son was Daniel born 1661 who married Rachel Fell in 1682/3 at Swarthmoor. Margaret Fox originally opposed the match on the grounds of difference of ages, Rachel was eight years older. In 1691 he resolved the family dispute by buying every other claimant out principally his nephew Charles Fell but also all his sisters in law and their husbands and his mother in law Margaret Fox. Daniel and Rachel had a number of children but only John 1687-1771 grew to maturity. John Abraham was on at least one occasion referred to as John Daniel Abraham. Daniel Abraham sells the ancestral land at Hauxwell in 1697.[74]

Quakers could be prosecuted for their beliefs until the Toleration Acts came into effect. They could also be prosecuted for failure to pay tythes. Daniel was a man of very tender conscience he refused to pay anything with the word church in it even if the proceeds did not go to the Church of England. In the spring of 1687 James II issued his Declaration of Indulgence for all Nonconformists It was brought in for the benefit of Roman Catholics and was resented for that reason.

However it gave Quakers freedom to worship as they chose. In 1689 William and Mary brought in the Toleration Act which had the same effect. However they were expected to be loyal to the crown and pay tithes. Failure to pay tithes could lead to imprisonment and confiscation of assets to pay the "debt". Daniel Abraham suffered in this respect from failure to pay rectory rents in Ulverston. [75]

In 1687 George Fox realising that Swarthmoor Hall might one day pass out of Quaker ownership took advantage of the Declaration of Indulgence to give to the Local Society of Friends the building at Petty Croft he had purchased from Susannah and Rachel Fell for £72. He appointed four step sons in law as trustees John Rous, Thomas Lower, William Mead and Daniel Abraham

Daniel Abraham was a man of very tender conscience. He participated in Quaker worship when it was illegal, he refused to pay tithes, he refused to pay fee farm rents believing they went to the priests salary. He was finally persuaded in 1699 that this was not so by his brothers in law, William Ingram and Thomas Lower. [76] He was imprisoned a number of times, fined a number of times and had livestock confiscated to pay the tithes. All this reduced his monetary wealth both directly and by preventing him from managing his business interests

In September 1683 Daniel Abraham his wife and mother in law were tried by Roger and William Kirby in Lancaster and sent to jail for absence from public worship. In June 1684 the three of them were back in jail. In 1701 he was in jail in Dalton for failure to pay tithes, he was there when Margaret Fox died in 1702. He was transferred to London by a writ of Habeous Corpus in 1704 and soon thereafter released

The sale of Hauxwell in 1697 indicates his financial difficulties and was followed by other sales. He tried to sell to friends or relatives or to other Quakers.[77] He sells land at Knott in Blawith in 1716.[78] He sells land at Bethicar in 1723. [79] In 1725 he sells land in Stable Harvey[80]. He with his son John is renting out land in Ulverston in 1729 and selling other land in the same year 81. Disposing of fields near the hall in 1730. [82] On the other hand there is evidence of income from manorial fees and elsewhere. As for instance the inheritance of a barn and garth in Soutergate by Hannah Fish in 1700 together with other fees in 1702, 1709/10 and 1718 as the tenancy changed hands. [83] He dies in 1731 and his wife Rachel in 1732. His son John is the only surviving child. He marries Sarah Foster in 1722. Sarah 1701-77 was the third daughter of Thomas and Sarah Foster of Hawthorn County Durham. They had four sons and seven daughters all born at the hall. He was apparently known as Lord Abraham.

John was said to have purchased the manor of Ulverston in 1718. [84] West in an account of the descent of the manor just says Mr Abraham who could be Daniel.

I find this somewhat surprising in view of the family's financial difficulties. Also there is the fact that the manor was transferred to Daniel Abraham in the tripartite indenture of 1691. The Neville Hall part of Ulverston manor probable coming into the family as early 1611.[85] It is possible the other half was purchased from the Kirkby's by Judge Fell when the Kirkby family was experiencing financial difficulties.[86] Certainly it seems to disappears from the lists of Kirkby assets during Judge Fell's life time. The Manor of Ulverston features in a list of Richard Kirkby's assets in 1646 when his estate was suffering sequestration for being a royalist.

It was no longer in the Kirkby estate in 1689. The Manors of Swarthmoor, Ulverston and Osmotherly are all mentioned in George Fell's will in 1670. So the Manor of Ulverston was transferred from the Kirkbys to the Fell (possibly with intermediaries between 1646 and 1670). Thomas Fell was sequestrator of royalist estates and this may have given him opportunity to acquire this manor. Which may account for the perpetual hostility of The Kirkbys for the Fells and their descendants. Sarah Foster was an heiress, her brother Robert Foster will crop up later in the story. John and Sarah's children were:- Thomas 1723-78; Margaret 1726-83 who married Ebenezer Miller of Manchester; Daniel 1728-31; Robert 1729; Rachel 1732-1845; Sarah 1734-5; Sarah 1736-40; Mary 1737 married Charles Cannon of Manchester; Alice 1739-1803, Hannah 1741-1825; son 1741. Part of the marriage settlement between John Abraham and the Fosters at his marriage to Sarah was that £600 was to be provided for their younger children after John's death.[87]

In 1746 John handed over Swarthmoor Hall, three watermills in Ulverston and 250 acres of land to his eldest son Thomas but continued to live there while Thomas lived in Whitehaven.[88] Thomas agreed to take on his father's debts and to make himself liable to provide £600 for the benefit of John and Sarah's younger children after John's death. This £600 presumably arose either from John & Sarah's marriage settlement or later when the Fosters bailed John out. The £600 continued as a charge on the Swarthmoor Hall Estate for a while after the Abrahams sold out. Sarah would presumably benefit from the will of her uncle Robert Foster of Hawthorn whose heir was her brother Robert and whose executors included Warren Maude a butcher married to her sister Mary and Nicholas Dodgson who was either father-in-law or brother in law of her brother Robert.[89] John Abraham finally left Swarthmoor in 1759 when he moved to Skirton near Lancaster. He was brought back after death for burial at Sunbrick in 1771.[90]

Thomas Abraham also married an heiress in 1752. She was the daughter of Henry Clare of Martinscroft in South Lancashire. They had the following children :- John 1750, Henry Chetham 1751, Catherine 1752, Sarah 1755, Ellen 1758 Margaret 1760 Rachel 1762 Ann 1764, Robert 1766, Maria 1768, Thomas 1771 and Henry Clare 1775. The first nine were born at Whitehaven, Thomas was born at Seaton all dedicated at the local Quaker Meeting. Ellen brought Thomas £3000 nonetheless he went bankrupt in 1753 allegedly because of losses in the tobacco trade. He had been dealing with his brother in Nansendsound River in Virginia. Something went wrong with a cargo which was lost. However Thomas had other financial problems. The younger Thomas appears in the 1851 census as a labourer and in 1861 as a retired schoolmaster. He had married at St Andrew's Parish Church in Penrith in 1803 Orpah Clarke who father James Clarke had written a descriptive book about the Lakes *Survey of the Lakes*. There are letters from his relatives to each other expressing concern about how he was getting on. Their first Robert was baptised in 1804 at St Andrews, when he grew up he trained as a doctor, then took up the editorship of the *Whitehaven Gazette* and then emigrated to Montreal where he died in 1754.[91] Thomas and Orpah had a number of children some of them dedicated at the Carlisle Quaker Meeting.

Their son John A Abraham became a pharmaceutical chemist in Bold in Liverpool. He lived in Grassendale Park in Liverpool. On a visit to the Lakes while staying at Lowick, he visited Ulverston and was asked if he was any connection of Lord Abraham. So he went to look at Swarthmoor Hall and persuaded Mrs Salthouse the widow of the late tenant to put him up for the night. He didn't enjoy the experience but it set off an interest in the Hall and his background which was taken up by his daughter Ellen Clarke Abraham.[92]

John A Abraham married Mary Hayes Tyerman in Liverpool in 1844. They had a number of children including Emma Clark and Thomas Fell Abraham who was also a pharmaceutical chemist and was the father of Edward Mitford Abraham who succeeded Emma Clarke at Swarthmoor and Isabel who married William MacGregor Ross and lived at Swarthmoor Hall for five years one of whose sons managed to take an aerial photograph of the hall using a kite. It is a useful photograph as it gives a good view of the long barn which has since been demolished. Isabel Ross wrote a book on Margaret Fell's life and works

John and Thomas Abraham had financial difficulties. This may be because they were paying fines for non attendance at church. They may have had livestock and other movable property seized for refusing to pay tithes, though the worst of the hardships should have ceased after the *Toleration Acts*. Or they may have been bad or unfortunate in business. There is long history of sales mortgages of land and assets leading up to Thomas's bankruptcy in 1753. Though John was able to stay at Swarthmoor till the property was sold to new owners in 1759. Daniel Abraham had already being selling property starting apparently with the Fell family estate of Hauxwell.

In 1728 John Abraham mortgages a house he had built at Lane Side between Dragley Beck and West End to James Barrow of Upper Newton in Cartmel.[93]

In 1729 he sells Cockhole and Hodbarrow (which he had previously bought from his father) to Thomas Brockbank. [94] He also sold land in Osmotherley to Thomas Millerson. [95] In 1729 he and his father Daniel Abraham mortgage land viz:- two Lund Meadows (4 acres), Star Meadow, two Whitwell Meadows (5 acres), Great Coalland, Stile Close, West End Meadow and West End Close to William Bordley.[96] They must have paid this mortgage off as some of these lands are available for sale or mortgage later on. However in 1740 there is an assignment from William Bordley to Nicholas Dodgson and Warren Maude.[97]

In 1730 John mortgages four fields viz:- Harrison Close (2 acres) Anglessea (2 acres) Ragnald Holm (2 acres 3 roods) and Dodham Wife Close (2 acres) to James Barrow of Upper Newton-in-Cartmel.[98] In 1731 he collects manorial fees relating to Newland Mill, in 1733 he mortgages a water corn mill called Town Mill to William Kirkby of Ashlack. [99] In 1735 John mortgages Swarthmoor Hall and a water corn mill and the Over Milne to James Barrow of Upper Newton for £300.[100] After this Abraham and Barrow assign the same to Robert Forster of Hawthorn County Durham,[101] followed by an assignment from Barrow to Nicholas Dogeson and Warren Maude.[102] In 1736 he mortgages all his Ulverston property to his brother in law Robert Forster of Hawthorn.[103] In October 1736 having mortgaged the manor to a Mr Harrison he sold the manor to a Mr Dummer who a fortnight later (4th,11th,12th November) sold the manor to the Duke of Montagu and subsequently became his agent.[104] Abraham required the consent of a Mr Harrison to whom he had already mortgaged his property.

In 1737 he sells the Old Chemists shop to Dr Stephen Fell a fellow Quaker and a doctor. It is possible he sold the adjacent shop now a hairdresser's to Stephen's brother James.[105] By 1739 John Abraham's brother-in-law Robert Forster had died, his heir was his nephew Robert Forster of Hawthorn and his executors were Nicholas Dodgson gentleman Hawthorn who was either the heirs father-in-law or his brother in law, Warren Maude butcher of Sunniside Bishop Wearmouth who was married to Sarah Abraham's sister Mary, Edward Walton and Eleazor Wardell. In the event Watson and Wardell decline to act as executors.

In 1739 Robert Forster the nephew sells his claim on John Abraham's land to his uncle's remaining executors Dodgson and Maude they enter a bill of complaint to the High Court of Chancery to compel John Abraham either to pay or forfeit the land the principal and interest now standing at £7269-9-4.[106] To meet this John Abraham took a loan of £6000 from Sir William Wentworth of Bretton Hall West Riding of Yorkshire by mortgage on Swarthmoor Hall and all other messuages mill etc and again misses the repayment date.[107] To meet some of his obligations he and his son Thomas sell Great Clott Land at Dragley Beck, Little Clott Land, Two Whitwell Meadows, Starr and Lund Meadow, Barnbeck, West End Close and

West End Meadow to John Dodson gentleman Ulverston for £675-9-0. All this is sealed in a fourway indenture of 1747 between Wentworth, the two Abrahams and John Dodson.[108] In 1740 he sells Great Dales, Long Dales and Little Greedy Ford to Richard Backhouse carpenter.[109] In 1743 he has a mortgage from James Collins of Knaresbrough re cottages in Ulverston and Manchester and elsewhere in Lancashire.[110] In 1759 Collins sells this mortgage to Henry Bainbridge also of Knaresbrough.[111] In 1748 John Abraham in conjunction with his son Thomas sells fields near Dragley Beck.[112] In May 1752 Thomas Abraham mortgages the hall three water corn mills in Ulverston and all his other property in Ulverston to Peter Nicholson then of Dublin with a redemption value of £1785 113. Thomas is living in Whitehaven but his father is living at the hall. In June 1752 Nicholson sells his interest to Matthias Gale[114] and John Bell of London.[115] By February 1753 Thomas owes Nicholson a further £285 while Gale and Bell are owed £2463.[116] In January 1759 Anthony Ponsonby of Whitehaven pays Gale and Bell £2543 at the request of Thomas Abraham and Peter Nicholson and Ponsonby acquires a years lease on the hall 25 fields and the three water mills.[117]

In February 1759 after the bankruptcy of Thomas Abraham, John Gale and Edmund Gibson both of Whitehaven of the commission of bankruptcy for Thomas Abraham indemnify John Law of Ulverston with a bond of £1000 against any claims of John and Sarah Abraham concerning lands formerly in the possession of the said John Abraham and later in possession of Thomas Abraham grocer Whitehaven bankrupt and now in the possession of Thomas Petty who holds the lands solely for transmission to the several purchasers including Dodgeson Close sold by Petty to John Law.[118] There is a similar bond indemnifying John Jackson of Ulverston regarding the purchase of Kirby Gill at Ulverston.[119] In 1757 John Lewthwaite and Peter Gale assignees of the commission of bankruptcy invite Alexander Hoskins to take a hand. Thomas Abraham is the nominal owner of the hall though not resident. His father is still in residence and Thomas now owes Sir William Wentworth £5774-9-9 on the mortgage Thomas is already bankrupt and declines to pay off his mortgage. Alexander Hoskins pays out £2000 to Sir William the remaining £3774-9-9 being secure by an indenture of release on the land from Hoskins to Wentworth. Peter Nicholson agrees to pay £5774-9-9 by the eleventh of November 1757. Peter Nicholson being still owed £1785 by Thomas Abraham.[120]

As early as December 1749 Thomas Abraham had advertised the Swarthmoor Hall Estate for sale with grounds, 200 acres of farmland with two good farm-houses on it, three water corn mills in Ulverston and a tenanted shop in Ulverston Market Place rented out at £3 per annum. Enquiries to Thomas Abraham esquire of Whitehaven or James Collins attorney at law of Knaresbrough. Only two months before he had married Ellen Clare at Penketh Quaker Meeting. Ellen had a fortune of £5000. A further advertisement in the London Evening Post between 21st December 1751 and 7th January 1752.[121] The two farms are named and described as Low Farm with messuage and outbuildings and 50 acres let at £70 a year and Curwin Farm with messuage and out buildings with 23 acres let at £30 a year. An extra agent was appointed Mr John Fell of Gray's Inn son of James Fell innholder. It is possible these two farms are the buildings at either end of the long barn. Thomas went bankrupt in March 1753.

In May the creditors of Thomas Abraham and other bankrupts were invited to meet the assignees of their estates at the sign of the Indian King in Whitehaven. In September 1755 his assets were divided into three tranches of which the first was Swarthmoor Hall, the second a sum of money due under the will of Robert Forster his uncle and the third were a number of properties at Halton, Poulton and Rixton all near Warrington and may represent ancestral Abraham assets or possibly assets brought to the marriage by Ellen Clare.

A seven part indenture of 9th February 1759 worked out by Thomas Petty settled what could be settled. When Thomas Abraham went bankrupt George Irton, Edmund Gibson, Hugh Holme, William Milbourne and John Park were appointed a commission of bankruptcy and John Lewthwaite and Peter Gale were appointed as assignees of the estate.[122] Further Peter Nicholson was declared bankrupt in 1754 his commission of bankruptcy was Andrew Huddleston, William Milbourn, George Irton, Edmund Gibson and Anthony Ponsonby and Matthias Gale was the assignee of the commission for the estate. Thomas Petty picks up the burden of £600 for John Abraham's younger children having offered £9675/16/- for the whole estate at the sale by the assignees of Thomas Abraham. Petty pays Alexander Hoskins £6411/13/-, Henry Bainbridge £945/13/- and Anthony Ponsonby £2317/10/- with 5/- each to Thomas Abraham John Lewthwaite, Peter Gale and Peter Nicholson.

The three water corn mills are sold in 1759 to a consortium ropery consisting of James Machell of Hollow Oak James Backhouse of July Flower Tree gentlemen, John Dodgeson and James Fell mariners and William Noble ropemaker. Fell buys the Over Mill in 1763 and Machell the Town Mill in 1764.The Abrahams left Swarthmoor Hall. In 1759

However on 2nd April 1764 John Abraham brought an action against his son and his son's creditors to assert that he had conveyed ownership of Swarthmoor Hall sometime previously.[123]

1. John Abraham and Sarah his wife paupers

2. Alexander Hoskins, James Collins, Edmund Gibson, John Lowthwaite, Peter Nicholson, Peter Gale, Matthias Gale, Thomas Abraham and Zachary Hubbersty

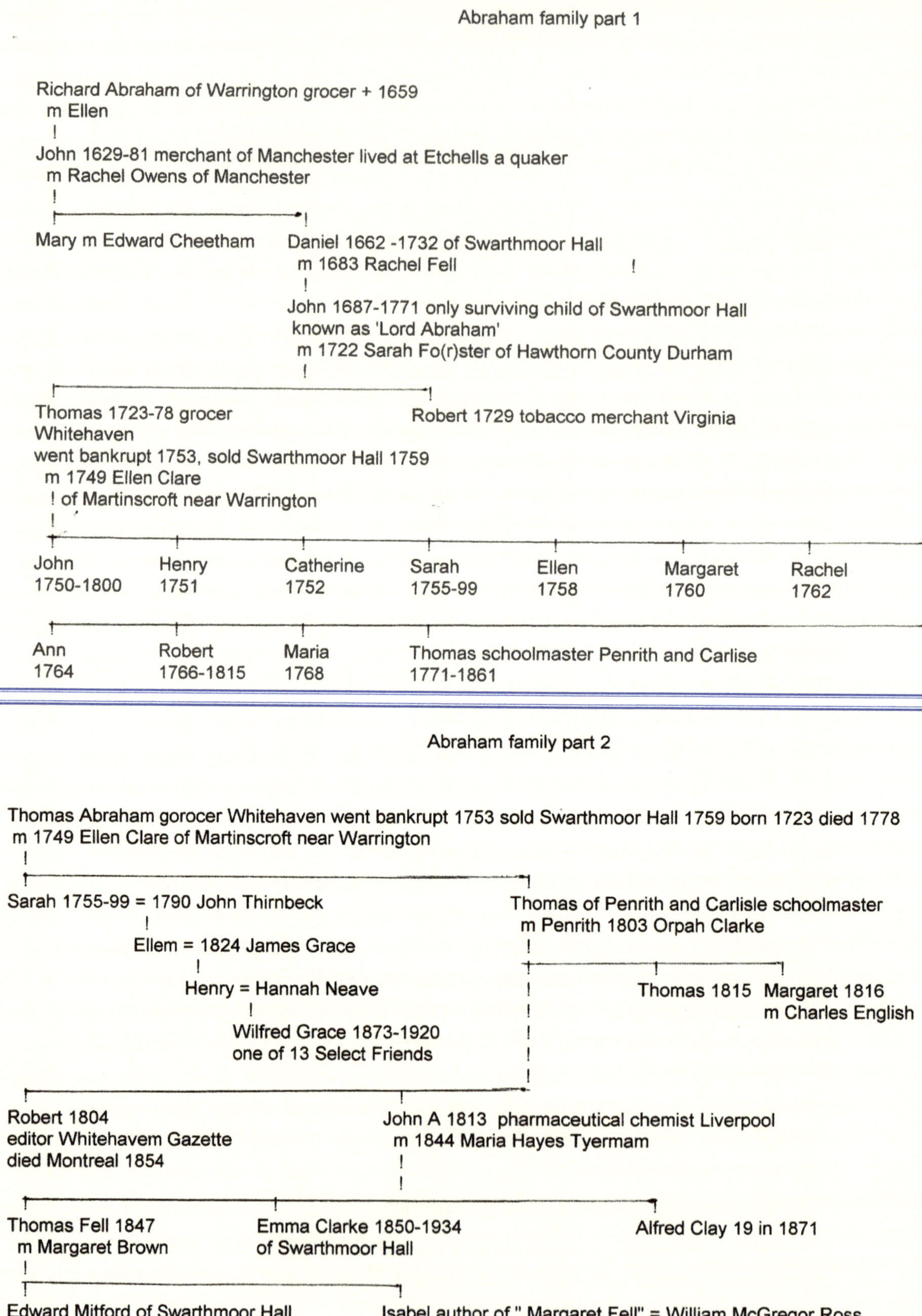

Abraham family part 1

Richard Abraham of Warrington grocer + 1659
m Ellen

John 1629-81 merchant of Manchester lived at Etchells a quaker
m Rachel Owens of Manchester

Mary m Edward Cheetham

Daniel 1662 -1732 of Swarthmoor Hall
m 1683 Rachel Fell

John 1687-1771 only surviving child of Swarthmoor Hall
known as 'Lord Abraham'
m 1722 Sarah Fo(r)ster of Hawthorn County Durham

Thomas 1723-78 grocer
Whitehaven
went bankrupt 1753, sold Swarthmoor Hall 1759
m 1749 Ellen Clare
of Martinscroft near Warrington

Robert 1729 tobacco merchant Virginia

John 1750-1800
Henry 1751
Catherine 1752
Sarah 1755-99
Ellen 1758
Margaret 1760
Rachel 1762
Ann 1764
Robert 1766-1815
Maria 1768
Thomas schoolmaster Penrith and Carlise 1771-1861

Abraham family part 2

Thomas Abraham gorocer Whitehaven went bankrupt 1753 sold Swarthmoor Hall 1759 born 1723 died 1778
m 1749 Ellen Clare of Martinscroft near Warrington

Sarah 1755-99 = 1790 John Thirnbeck

Ellem = 1824 James Grace

Henry = Hannah Neave

Wilfred Grace 1873-1920
one of 13 Select Friends

Thomas of Penrith and Carlisle schoolmaster
m Penrith 1803 Orpah Clarke

Thomas 1815

Margaret 1816
m Charles English

Robert 1804
editor Whitehavem Gazette
died Montreal 1854

John A 1813 pharmaceutical chemist Liverpool
m 1844 Maria Hayes Tyermam

Thomas Fell 1847
m Margaret Brown

Emma Clarke 1850-1934
of Swarthmoor Hall

Alfred Clay 19 in 1871

Edward Mitford of Swarthmoor Hall
m Dorothy Allard

Isabel author of " Margaret Fell" = William McGregor Ross

Hugh

Peter

A recap may be helpful. John Abraham mortgages Swarthmoor Hall to his uncle in law Robert Foster. Robert Foster dies and his nephew Abraham's brother in law inherits. He passes the benefit of the loan to two of his uncles executors Nicholas Dodgson and Warren Maude. Meanwhile John has handed his interest in the hall to his son Thomas. Thomas is sued by Dodgson and Maude and takes a loan from Sir William Wentworth for £6000. He sells his interest to Matthias Gale and John Bell both of London. They sell their interest to Anthony Ponsonby who is compensated by Thomas Petty. Also Thomas Abraham borrows money from Peter Nicholson on the security of the three watermills (already mortgaged to Wentworth) and land etc in Manchester. Peter Nicholson passes his interest to Alexander Hoskins who is compensated by Thomas Petty. There is the mortgage to James Collins who passes his rights onto Henry Bainbridge who is paid out by Thomas Petty. It is possible Petty kept Thomas Abraham out of jail.

EXCURSUS VI
OTHER RESIDENTS AT SWARTHMOOR 1691-1753

James Fell husbandman Swarthmoor acts as bondsman for a marriage license in 1698/9

George Seale of Swarthmore acts as bondsman for a marriage license for Elizabeth Seale and George Fell of Ulverston in 1701/2

Ann Fell of Swarthmoor has a license to marry 1702

George Sheriff gardener Swarthmoor Hall has a license to marry Sarah Fisher in 1724, the bondsman Roger Whinfield is said to be of the same place but whether this refers to Swarthmoor or Ulverston is not clear

Martin Mackintosh and Alice Benson were both of Swarthmoor when they obtained a license to marry, their bondsman Thomas Callender was also of Swarthmoor

CHAPTER FOUR
THE LINDOWS

Lindow (variously spelt Lindow, Lindowe, Lindo, Lindoe) was a common name in Ulverston and surrounding areas and at one stage virtually every farm or hamlet in the area bounded by the A590, the A 5094 and the B5281 had Lindow residents. The particular settlement we are interested in is Topping Rays which is about half a mile North-northeast of Arrad Foot and slightly further from Greenodd.

Robert Lindowe of Toppingraise's will was both made and proved in 1590. However the first person we can connect with the Lindows who bought Swarthmoor Hall is Thomas Lindow of Nether Scathwaite who made his will in 1697 (proved1699). He had a wife Elizabeth and two daughters Ann Kendall and Ellen Lindowe. His brother William Lindow of Toppingraise was a trustee. William was a showmaker. An application for a meeting place for dissenters at Topping Raise was made in 1692. In 1707 He leaves his timber and boards and husbandry gear to his eldest son John and the residue to his wife Elizabeth and son John. Also mentioned are a younger son James, daughter Ann Carter, Sarah Shaw, Elizabeth Lindow and Agnes Capeland, Two brother's in law George Taylor and William Harrison.

There are two nearly contemporary wills for men called John Lindow of Topping Raise. However the one who made his will in 1718 (proved 1719) is the one that is in sequence He leaves Topping Raise to his brother James Lindow yeoman plus other unspecified land in Egton cum Newland on condition he pays £40 to each of his sisters Ann Jackson, Sarah Shaw, Elizabeth Frearson and Agnes Coupland together with a number of other bequests including one to Mr Thomas Richardson dissenting minister of Ulverston..

James makes his will in 1737 (proved 1741) he refers to himself as mariner of Topping Rays Ulverston. His principle heir is his eldest son William, not yet of age who gets land buildings etc in Toppingrays in Ulverston and elsewhere in Lancashire./ His executor is his wife Elizabeth who gets the residue. Provision is made for three other children Ellen, Agnes and James all under age. Captain James has already started buying land from the Swarthmoor Hall estate. There exists a map labelled "draft of the part of Swarthmoor Hall Estate bought for Captain James Lindow"[125]

Nothing seems to been done about this proposed sale as the various lands mentioned were still in the hands of the Abrahams after James's will was proved. James had married Elizabeth Hull in 1717. James died in Dublin in 1741, his funeral service was at Tottlebank.

William was born at Toppingrays and baptised at Ulverston in 1724. His sister Ellinor had been born in Soutergate and baptised Ulverston 1720. He married Abigail Rawlinson of Lancaster and settled in Lancaster. They had no children. Thomas Abraham was trying to sell Swarthmoor Hall. It was advertised in 1749, 1750 and 1751. It was put up for auction in 1752. Thomas went bankrupt in 1753. The Hall was again offered for sale in 1755. Thomas Petty was appointed receiver of Thomas Abraham's bankrupt estate. In 1759 James Jackson hatter bought Swarthmoor from Thomas Petty using William Lindow's money and acting as his attorney but buying in his own name as Lindow was out of the country. By 1761 Lindow had returned and Swarthmoor Hall and estate was transferred to him. As well as Swarthmoor Hall and its supporting buildings. Lindow purchased :- [126] *see Excursus 5*

William Lindow at one stage owned 22 & 24 Soutergate Ulverston. This may be where his sister Ellinor was born. One of these houses has a gutter inscribed W L 1757. His father was a mariner and sea captain. He followed into the trade He invested in a slave trip with Moses Benson and Postlethwaite. He went to Lancaster as a merchant in the slave trade working with Abraham Rawlinson and Thomas Hutton Rawlinson Quaker slave traders. William Lindow was sent to Grenada in the 1660s by the Rawlinsons to be their agent there. He also worked on St Kitts as a factor He became a partner of the Rawlinsons.[127] He was appointed to the Governor's Counsel of Grenada in 1765. In place of Mr Cargill who had died.

In 1769 the British Government wished to make the French settlers in Grenada feel they were citizens accordingly Frenchmen were appointed JPs in every parish, but there were no Frenchmen on the council which already had 12 members which was the maximum allowed by the constitution. Non the less Lt Governor Ulysses Fitzmaurice went ahead and appointed two Frenchmen Devaqconnu and Chanteloup. In protest at this Messers Graham, Lindow, Corsor, Melville, Townsend and Williams left the chamber and were subsequently suspended by Fitzmaurice in the absence of the governor. They were restored by order of the privy Council 5th April 1771 with the proviso that they were to be reprimanded by the governor at their restoration for their unjustifiable conduct.[128] The Council in 1770 consisted of: Francis Gore (Lt Governor, Robert Turner, John Graham, Patrick Maxwell, William Lindow, Frederick Corsor, John Harvey, Thomas Townsend, William Lucas, John Melville, Thomas Williams and Paul Mignot Devuconnu. He returned to Lancaster and married Abigail Rawlinson in 1771. They lived in 1 Queen St in Lancaster. Their portrait was painted by Romney in 1772. They had a black slave called John Chance.

His sister Agnes married Brian Christopherson and his sister Ellenor married James Jackson. In 1665 or thereabout the three brothers in law bought Wellhead at Ulverston in order to open a soap works. They soon sold out again as their product didn't sell very well. In his will (Appendix I) in 1787 he describes himself as merchant of Lancaster and he owned land at Bank End in Ulverston, Arrad Foot, Topping Raise and Oxenhouse together with land in Tobago, Dominica, And Grenada and plantations in Grenada and St Vincent. His heirs were his sisters and their families brother James having died young. Swarthmoor Hall was left to trustees John Bowes esquire Lancaster, James Lucas esquire of Hulton near Preston and Jackson Mason gentleman Lancaster with the income to go to his niece Ann Jackson daughter of his sister Ellinor and her husband James Jackson hatter. After Ann's death the hall was to go to her eldest son and failing him younger sons in age order and failing all of them to her daughters in age order. Ann died in 1823 and the Hall came into the hands of William Lindow Dickinson.

As James Jackson hatter and feltmaker held the hall for two years as Lindow's attorney and as further he had married Lindow's sister Eleanor and it was his grandson William Lindow Dickinson who eventually inherited, it might be as well to say what was known about him.

In 1754 he had bought a parcel of moss near Oubas Hill from Thomas Petty who was acting as receiver for the Swarthmoor estate.[129] In 1764 he took Agnes Tatill as an apprentice to learn housewifery.[130] He had married Eleanor Lindow in 1755. Ann was born in 1759. They had two other children James and Elizabeth both of whom died young. For a time at any rate James Jackson and Ellinor his wife were of Bank End. Ann Jackson married at Broughton-in-Furness in 1786 William Dickinson a surgeon who came from a medical family originating near Whitehaven. William and Ann had the following children baptised at Broughton :- Eleanor 1786, William Lindow 1788, Joseph Stamper 1789; Frances 1791 and Ann 1793

Neither James Jackson nor William Lindow nor William Lindow Dickinson nor William Lindow Fletcher seems to have lived at the hall. It was either empty or tenanted during the whole Lindow period. At the end of this section there is a list of who lived at the hall sometimes specifically said to have done so and others described as living at Swarthmoor which contained very few dwellings other than those at the hall. The farms attached to the estate had already been let out by Thomas Abraham.

A William Lindow, mariner, of Lancaster purchased his freedom of Lancaster for 5gns in 1752/3[131] In 1757 William Lindow, mariner, of Topping Raise sells wood growing on land he owns at Arrad Foot to Sir Edward Montague. In 1763 James Jackson, hatter, Ulverston; William Lindow, merchant, Ulverston; John Jackson, farmer, Stainton Gap & Thomas Townson, yeoman, Pennington acquire from William Singleton of Drigg a lease of 21 years allowing to search for and extract lead, copper, tin or iron in the waste land of the Manor of Ulpha and to create ancillary premises suitable to the exercise.[132]

In 1765 William Lindow buys Oxenhouse from James Jackson.[133] In 1766 William Lindow, then in Grenada, sold part of Highbridge Meadow to Thomas Petty to transfer to various purchasers.[134]

In 1783 William Lindow buys Bank End in Broughton-in-Furness from Thomas Stanley and is admitted as a customary tenant of the Manor of Broughton-in-Furness.[135] In 1771 William Lindow buys a messuage, tenement and tithe at Channonhouse Pennington from Thomas Townson.[136]

In 1787 Abigail Lindow widow of William comes to an arrangement allowing James Jackson and Eleanor his wife to continue living at Bank End Broughton.[137]

From 1787 till 1823 The hall was in the hands of trustees. The initial trustees were John Bowes of Lancaster, James Lucas of Hulton near Preston, Jackson Mason of Lancaster However by 1808 William Dickinson of Workington (Ann's husband) was advertising for a tenant and citing his brother Daniel Dickinson attorney of Ulverston as a trustee.[138]

In 1823 The Hall was the property of William Lindow Dickinson who in a letter correctly states his relationship to William Lindow via his mother Ann Jackson Dickinson and her mother Eleanor Lindow Jackson sister to William Lindow. [139]

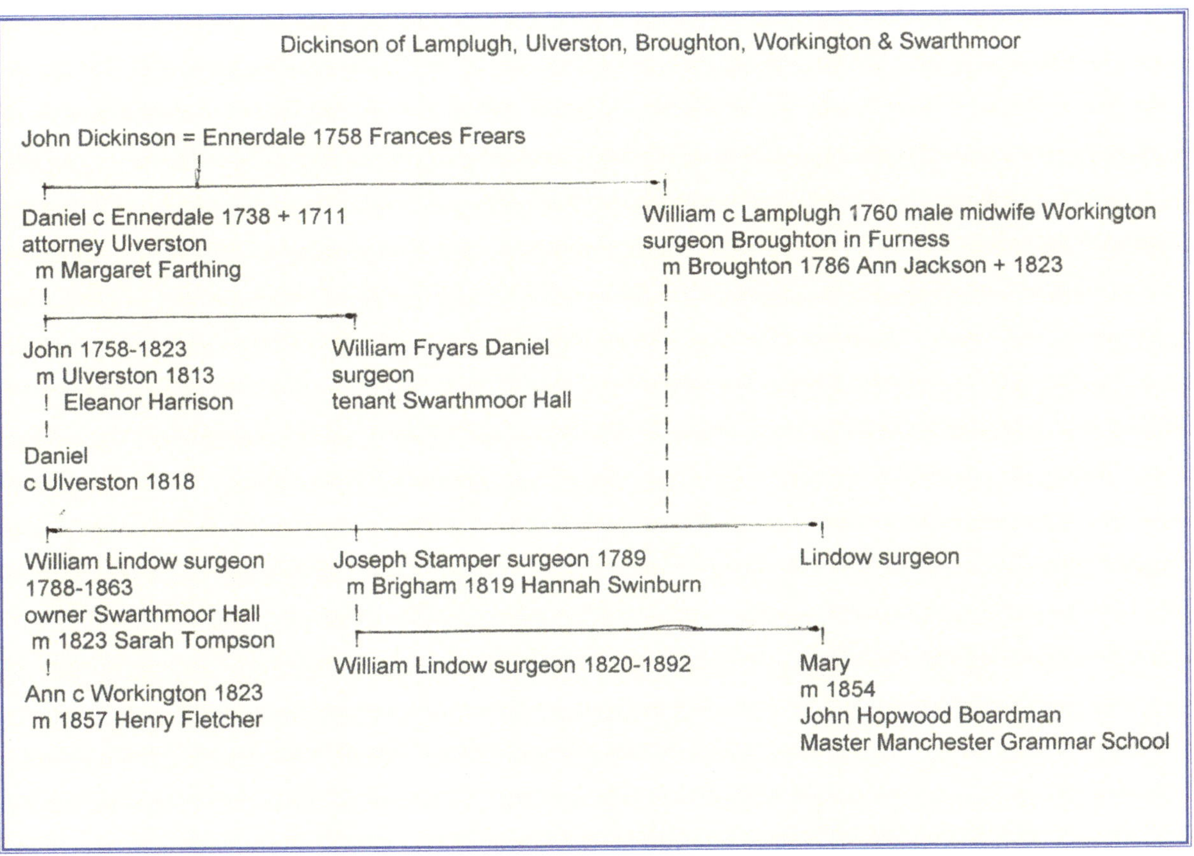

He marries at Brigham in 1723 Sarah Tompson and has two daughters Ann and Mary. Ann was born in 1826. Under William's will his wife Sarah gets the house and all his estate for life and widowhood. William dies in 1853 Ann marries in 1857 Henry Fletcher of Stoneleigh near Workington. They have three children Annie 1858, Amy 1861 and William Lindow Fletcher 1864 Under Thomas Fell's will money's had been set aside of which the interest went to pay for a schoolmaster, to clothe one apprentice per year, to pay for a few poor boys to have schooling. These various sums had mutated into a rent charge on the estate which was acknowledged by Mrs Ann Fletcher and handled by her tenant Francis Bennet[140] so evidently Mrs Fletcher followed her mother as owner of the hall passing it on in due course to her son William Lindow Fletcher who sold the hall to Emma Clark Abrahams.

Lindow of Topping Raise

Thomas Lindow of Nether Scathwaite will 1697/9
m Elizabeth

- Ann
  m Ulverston 1691
  John Kendall
  of Cockenshell
- Alice
  m Ulverston 1698
  Myles Dodgson of Scales
- Elizabeth

William of Topping Raise will 1707
m Elizabeth

- John will 1719
  of Topping Raise
- Ann
  m Robert Carter
  m John Jackson
- Sarah
  m Shaw

- Elizabeth
  m Lancelot Frearson
- Agnes
  m Coupland
- James of Topping Raise will 1737/41
  ship's captain
  attempted to buy land at Swarthmoor
  m Ulverston 1717/8 Elizabeth Hull

Lindow of Swarthmoor

James Lindow ship's captain Topping Raise will 1737/41 attempted to purchase land adjacent to Swarthmoor Hall
m Ulverston 1717 Elizabeth Hull

- Ellinor 1720
  m Ulverston 1735
  James Jackson hatter, feltmaker
  nominee owner Swarthmoor Hall
  - Elizabeth 1757
  - Ann 1759
    m Broughton in Furness 1786
    William Dickinson surgeon
    - William Lindow Dickinson surgeon owner Swarthmoor Hall
      1783-1853 of Workington
      m 1823 Sarah Tompson
      - Ann c Workington 1826
        m 1857 Henry Fletcher magistrate Stoneleigh Workington
        - Ammy 1858
        - Annie 1861
        - William Lindow Fletcher b 1861 sold Swarthmoor Hall 1912
          m 1912 Margaret Stordy
- William 1724-86 of Grenada & Lancaster
  owner Swarthmoor Hall
  m 1767 Abigail Rawlinson
- Agnes
  m Ulverston 1753
  Brian Christopherson
  - James 1761-1765
  - William 1755
  - Elizabeth 1759
    m Robt Carr
    of Liverpool
- James

EXCURSUS VII

WILLIAM LINDOW'S PURCHASE

The Avery a piece of ground planted with trees,

The Coppice planted with fir and other trees measuring three acres three roods and thirty perches adjoining the Foldyard of the hall;

Dickey Croft adjoining the coppice on the northwest containing nine acres and fourteen perches;

Bernard Field of eight acres, three roods twenty seven perches adjoining the west side of Dickey Croft;

All Low Bridge Meadows except that part lying on the north and north-east side of the rivulet which is in the possession of Robert Backhouse;

A field called Dragley abutting the east of the Coppice of six acres, three roods,m six perches and Old Wife Close adjoining the northeast of the Coppice of five acres one rood nineteen perches.

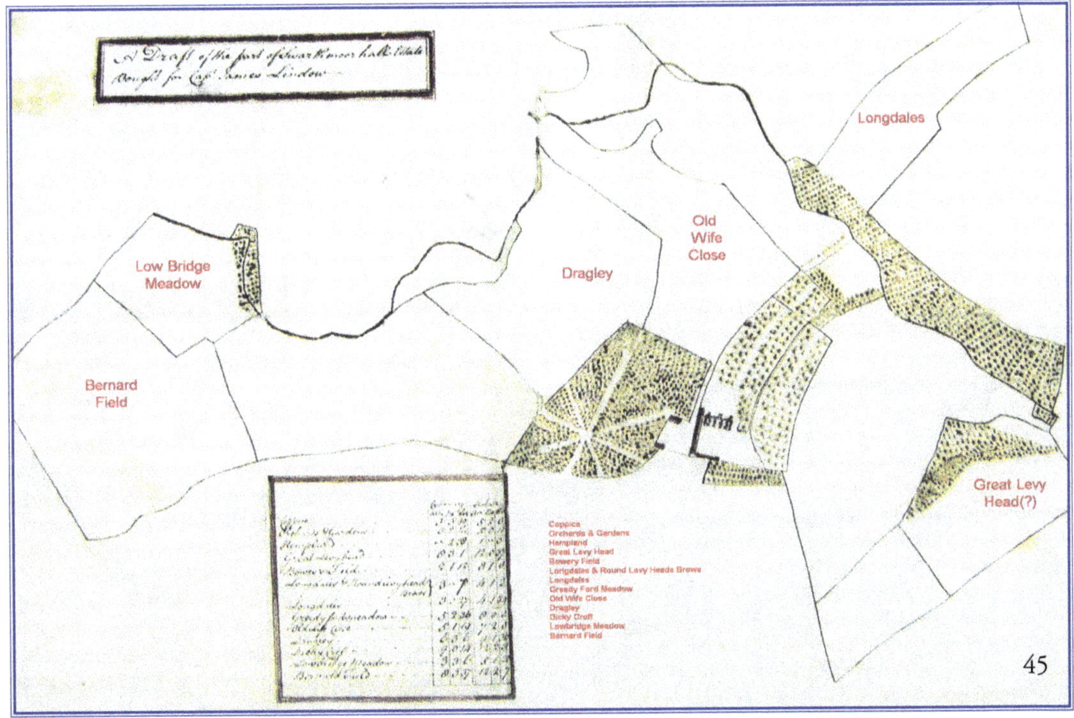

Greedy Ford Meadow adjoining north side Old Wife Close of five acres, two rood, thirtysix perches

Longdales adjoing the lane from Ulverston to Swarthmoor Common with the east end of three acres twentyseven perches

Parcel of woody ground called Longdales Brow and Levyheads adjoing east part thereof to Longdales

Field called Round Levyhead of x acres two roods seventeen perches except about six yards in breadth at the southeast side of Levyheads Brow for all watering placesa from the said Round Levyheads and the same is now or was formerly hedged off;

Great Levyheads Close of eight acres three roods and and one perch abutting west on the orchard and gardens belonging to the said Harrison

Harpenshaw of four acres one rood and one perch northwest of Great Levyheads

Bowes's Field abutting northeast of Harpenshaw of two acres, one rood & twelve perches

Hedges and fences of and belonging the said closes or adjoining the highway and common and from the bathing place in Dragley and downwards between that place and Old Wife Close and the Holmes

Two pews in Ulverston Church at the foot of the old gallery

West and moiety or lot of Rain Hill Moss in Ulverstone Moss divided from the part purchased by Thomas Chamney

Abraham Manuscript MS 5161364 page 51 which is at Friends House.

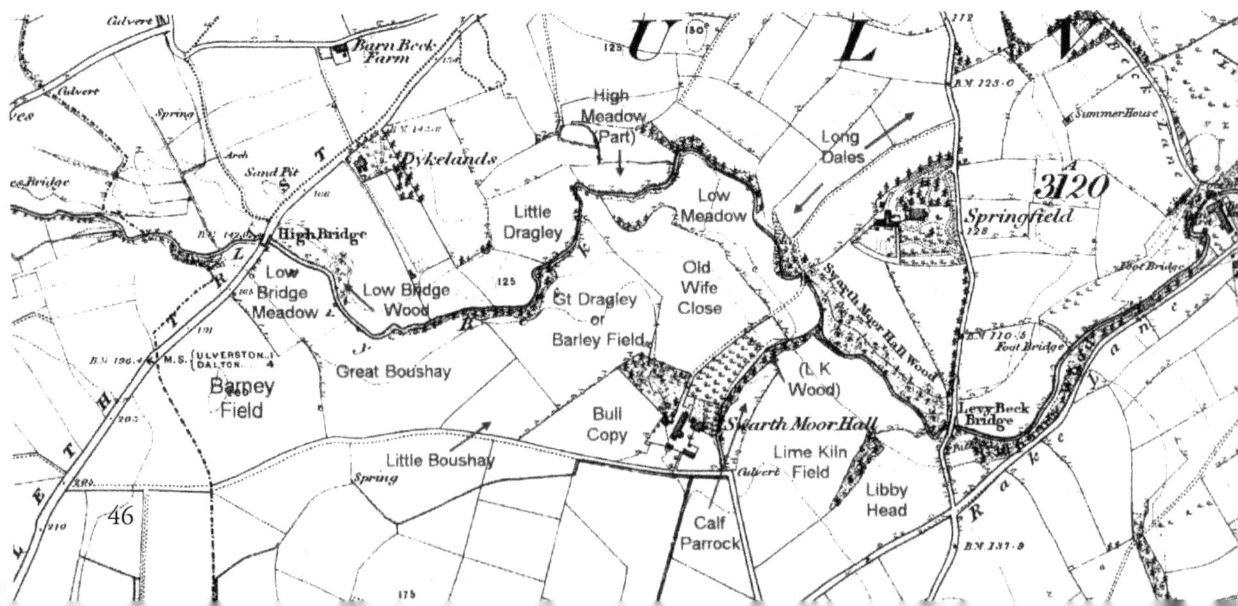

List drawn up on 13th June 1746 by John Abraham of properties he was willing to sell:

Ansley Lot
Renny Holl
Dodgson Wife Close
Allotment in the town
One shop in Ulverston rented out
Three mills in Ulverston
Barnbeck Close
Long Meadow & Whitewill Meadow
Farm called Colthouse Farm stables etc and 30 acres
Two Little Coat Lands
Two Great Coat Lands
Lane farm new house
West End Close and meadow
Nether Blundell Field
The Stile Close
Great Gule Croft
Great Widow House
High Little Widow Close
Lower Little Widow Close
Starr Meadow
Lund Meadow
High Bridge Meadow
Broad Dale
Benson Great Meadow
Benson Little Meadow
Copt Close Meadow
Hew Close
Stone Rigg
Addison's Close
The Parrock
Part of the Moss
With all of which he hoped to raise £5310

List of Lands John Abraham wished to keep:

Coppy fold and Wood
Dicky Croft
The Great Bosses
Low Bridge Meadow
Allettson's Close
Gutterstone and Gillerland Meadow
Holmes
Spittle Pot
Dragley
Old Wife Close
Great Ford Meadow
Little Ford Meadow Close
Great Dales
Long Dales
Little Levy Heads
Harrison Close
Round Levy Heads
Great Levy Heads
Harpenshaw
The Hempland
Kerby Wood
Fold or Yard

EXCURSUS VIII
THE TENANTS

Between 1763 and 1912 Swarthmoor was owned by the Lindow family. None of them actually lived there as far as we know. There were a succession of tenants. The chief features of the building were the hall itself with an adjacent long barn which seemed to have a double fronted house at each end. These are clearly visible on the photograph Peter Ross took by attaching a camera to a kite.. In addition part of the hall was known as the cottage. This comprises the room on the left of the central entrance passage and a room above. At one time the house nearest the road was used as a farm office but later on the wall between this house and the barn was taken down to allow for a larger barn. The rest includes a number of smaller barns and other out buildings none used for human habitation. There were no houses near the hall which were not part of the hall complex. Indeed the nearest habitation was at Petty Croft where George Fox built a meeting house. This small hamlet must have compromised all the rest of the habitation reckoned to be in Swarthmoor unless houses and their remains had disappeared prior to the 1855 ordnance map.

I am arranging the tenants and other inhabitants of the hamlet in chronological order[141]

Edward Benson recorded at Swarthmoor in Ulverston Court Roll for 1753

John Abraham finally left Swarthmoor in 1759.

However in June 1755 John Kellett formerly of Swarthmoor Hall, late of Hammerside Hill both in the parish of Ulverston gardener, salt maker and yeoman was being held in Lancaster Castle as a prisoner for debt.[142]

Ann Fell and Thomas Woodburn both of Swarthmoor were married in 1692.

In 1685/6 Alice daughter Edward and Ann Fell of Swarthmoor was both baptised and buried.

In 1709 was baptised Agnes daughter of James Fell of Swarthmoor.

In 1763 and 1766 James and Isaac son of Henry Woodburn of Swarthmoore were baptised.

In 1767 Thomas son of James Fell of Swarthmoor was baptised.

In 1768 burial of Frances Holme widow of Swarthmoor Hall

In 1769 Thomas Tyson husbandman Swarthmoor Hall takes Matthias Atkinson as an apprentice.[143] At some stage in the eighteenth century he is buying a messuage ar Mansriggs and another at Broughton Beck plus a pew in Ulverston Church from the executors and trustees estate of William Benson of Mansriggs who died in 1769. 144 From 1764 to 1772 he is a tenant of William Lindow at Swarthmoor Hall.[145]

In 1772 he is followed as a tenant by Robert Gorill who is paying rent in 1777

John Tyson of Swarthmoor has a daughter Peggy baptised 1772 and a daughter Agnes in 1775.

Robert Gorrill of Swarthmoor has two daughters Betty aged 3 and Dolly baptised in 1775. He left a will in 1796 when he was at Upper Greaves Pennington. He had a wife Martha, sons Robert, Edward, Christopher, daughters Margaret wife of Thomas Danson, Agnes wife of Stanyon Brigg, Betty, Dorothy, Martha wife of David Bradley and Nancy wife of William Wedderburn. Nancy had a son before marriage. John Gorrell, The younger Robert left a will in 1812 when at Castle Hill Pennington. He had a wife Hannah and apparently no children. At this time tenant farmers moved about a lot sometimes taking a new farm at the same time as the hiring fair

Also James Eccles als Heckles of Swarthmoor has six sons John, William, Thomas, Robert, Joseph and William baptised between 1762 and 1772. He had married Agnes Newby in 1755.

In 1771 Jane daughter Robert Ashburner of Swarthmoor was baptised.

In 1767 there was baptized Mary daughter James Doell of Swarthmoor.

In 1776 Fr Thomas West author of "The Antiquities of Furness moved into Swarthmoor Hall from Tytup Hall. In 1777 he moved again to the First House in Fountain St.[146] West was accused by Robert Abraham 1804-54 a great great grandson of Daniel and Rachel Abraham of deliberately excluding the Fells and Askews because they were Quakers. A charge which was attacked by J Brownbill.[147]

In 1779 was baptised Mary daughter of Thomas Hodgson of Swarthmoor Hall,

In 1787 Richard son Jonathan Wilson was baptised

In 1796 William Mainsty of Swarthmoor Hall was buried

In 1799 Thomas Coward farmer of Swarthmoor Hall was buried aged 69

In 1808 William Dickinson was advertising for a tenant for Swarthmoor Hall.

In 1812 and 1815 were baptised Elizabeth and Samuel children of Samuel and Ann Fell of the Nook Swarthmoor.

In 1820 Elizabeth daughter of William Sandham husbandman of Swarthmoor Hall and Elizabeth his wife was baptised.

In 1826 Frances Kipling Dixon daughter of Hugh Dixon farmer Swarthmoor Hall and his wife Ruth was baptised

In 1827 John Stephenson of Swarthmoor Hall married at Dalton Elizabeth Watson of Lindal

A deed of 1836 refers to John Coward of Swarthmoor Hall farmer and 12 enclosures in Swarthmoor in occupation of John Coward. [148]

By 1841 according to the census, the only residents at Swarthmoor Hall were an agricultural labourer William Sharp and his wife Margaret with two young daughters.

In 1845 John Abraham chemist of Liverpool visited Swarthmoor Meeting House, Sunbrick Graveyard and Swarthmoor Hall, being put up for the night by the then tenant a Mrs Salthouse. [149]

In 1847 Edward Johnson and John Johnson acquired some fields.[150]

In 1851 the census lists two farm labourers and their families Christopher Thompson from Kellington in Westmorland and his wife Margaret from Mossend in Cumberland :- James, Richard, Christopher, David & Thomas of whom only Thomas was born at Swarthmoor and Robert and Ann Mattinson with children Robert and Margaret evidently the family had the farm in hand to some extent during these years.

In 1853 Gulliver a pedigree shorthorn bull had been bred by Mr Dickinson at Swarthmoor Hall.[151] This was William Fryeear Daniel Dickinson a son of Daniel Dickinson attorney of Ulverston a brother of the William Dickinson who married Ann Jackson. He was actually living at 9 Fountain St in 1851 but was farming 160 acres which were evidently at Swarthmoor and presumably Thompson and Mattinson were working for him.

In 1854 F D Dickinson is selling Short horn cattle at Ulverston.[152]

In 1856 William Dickinson is offering the services of two shorthorn bulls 'Florian and; Cheddar' to serve cows at Swarthmoor Hall.[153]

In 1857 Sarah Dickinson wife of William Lindow Dickinson gives William Freer Daniel Dickinson surgeon notice to quit land belonging the Swarthmoor Hall estate and some of the buildings.[154] It is said he had been there nine years.

In the same year William Lindow Dickinson thanks William Fryear Daniel Dickinson for recommending Robert Slater as a tenant.[155] In 1858 Slater puts up a notice warning trespassers off the grounds of Swarthmoor Hall if they are out of the regular footpath.[156] In the 1861 census the tenant farmer is still Robert Slater who comes from Dalton and Sarah his wife with a daughter Agnes and three labourers.

In 1871 Andrew Birrell from Egton in Cumberland was farming His wife was from Aspatria and the following children Robert,Elizabeth, Nancy, Joseph, Margaret and a niece Nancy. The niece and three children were born at Lamplugh while the eldest was born at Brigham. There were two servants one born in Ulverston, the other at Cleator.

In 1881 Andrew and Margaret were still there with a nephew Adam Birrell from Lamplugh.

In 1891 Margaret was a widow with Adam as a farm labourer.but still at Swarthmoor, but also Francis Bennett was farming with Caroline his wife and four children Maud, William, Richard and Fanny two born at Grimsergh and two at Kirby Ireleth. Francis was an Ulverston man..

In 1901 Francis Bennett was still at the hall. Margaret Birrell had moved to Rosshead and Adam to Treadlea at Plumpton.

In 1911 Francis still at the hall was a widower, assisted by his son John Taylor Bennett.. Francis was still there when the hall and farm were put up for sale when Emma Clark Abraham bought it with help from thirteen Quakers.[157] A report of the sale appears in the Lancashire Post. The House and various parcels were initially auctioned as separate lots. The hall itself fetched £3500, four acres £700, nine acres £550 and eleven acres £275. The lots were then put together and fetched £5250 and was sold to Mr Lawrence R Wilson of Manchester who was acting on behalf of Dr Hodgkin of Newcastle for the English Society of Friends and Miss E. C Abraham of Liverpool The old oak bedstead fetched 15 guineas and remains at the hall.. Fox's desk however was sold for 26 guineas to Mrs Miles Kennedy of Stone Cross Ulverston.

CHAPTER FIVE

THE LATER ABRAHAMS AND THE SOCIETY OF FRIENDS

Emma Clark Abraham was the daughter of John A Abraham pharmaceutical chemist of Liverpool. She bought Swarthmoor Hall from Henry Lindow Fletcher in 1912.[158] She put up half the money herself and the other half was provided by 13 prominent Quakers. The arrangement was that Miss Abraham should have the use of the hall for her life and after her death it was to go to her nephew Edward Mitford Abraham and when he had no further use for it it would pass into the ownership and control of the Society of Friends Miss Abraham died in 1934. Mitford Abraham let his sister Isabel Ross her husband and two sons have the use of the hall for five years. He hands over in 1954.

Miss Abraham did a certain amount of restoration work replacing panelling which had been stripped. However there were innovations. The Liver Birds on the frieze in the great hall are from her. She built a two story extension on the North West corner and she added a balcony on the East frontage so that one could in theory step through the door onto the balcony. She thought she was restoring a historic feature believing that George Fox had used the balcony to preach to crowds outside. There is no contemporary evidence that George Fox did any such thing.

If the number of people attending Swarthmoor Hall was so large that they couldn't get into the great hall it is surprising the militia wasn't called. An alternative suggestion is that there was an outside staircase which enabled Judge Fell's customers to get to his office without going through the house. There is no contemporary evidence for this either. The most usual explanation for a door at that height is that it was a taking in door. The entrance Arch was built in 1914.

Isabel Ross her husband William McGregor Ross and their sons Hugh and Peter were the next residents. It was Peter McGregor Ross who took an aerial photograph of the hall using a kite. Mrs Ross was very hospitable. She also wrote *Margaret Fox mother of Quakerism*.

Mitford Abraham is responsible for the millstones which are distributed round the grounds. He was reported to have collected rents from houses in Woodlands Rd, Kilner Park Ulverston. This was probably because some of the houses had extended their gardens over Levy Beck or built bridges over it thus becoming tenants of the estate.

In 1954 the Society of Friends took over. One major change they made was to demolish the Long Barn and build a set of lecture rooms with some accommodation for visitors. They robbed out the foundations so the new building is not necessarily exactly on the same foot print. Some of old building remains below ground level. A recent excavation uncovered a curious structure. If one imagines two old fashioned beehives more or less conical but with the sides bulging out and inverts them, pushes them into the ground and replaces the construction material with stone corbelling and connect the two with a channel, that about describes the structure.

It is a pity the long barn was demolished without a thorough archaeological and architectural examination. The building goes back to James Lindow's lifetime as it appears on a map of properties they were thinking of selling to him. His will was proved in 1741. It would appear that the windows of at least one of the houses at either end had mullions. It is possible that one of these houses is the building in which George Fell Senior lived which was inherited by Thomas Fell.

— of —

Swarthmoor Hall Estate,

In the Parish of Ulverston, in the County of Lancaster,

CONTAINING UPWARDS OF

102 Acres of Arable, Pasture, Meadow & Woodland,

WITH SUITABLE BUILDINGS,

And including Valuable Building Sites,

SWARTHMOOR HALL.

To be Offered for Sale by Public Auction

BY

Mr. F. J. HARRISON, A.A.I.,

At the COUNTY AUCTION ROOMS, ULVERSTON,

On WEDNESDAY, the 28th day of August, 1912,

At 2-30 o'clock in the Afternoon.

Vendor's Agent: S. D. STANLEY-DODGSON, Esq., Somerset House, Whitehaven.
Vendor's Solicitors: Messrs. PAISLEY, FALCON, SKERRY & HIGHET, Workington.

Particulars.

LOT 1.

The Historical & Valuable Freehold Estate

KNOWN AS

"SWARTHMOOR HALL,"

Consisting of the Dwelling-house and Outbuildings and upwards of 77 acres in a ring fence of Arable, Pasture, Meadow, and Woodland, situate in the Parish of Ulverston, in the County of Lancaster, and now in the occupation of Mr. Francis Bennett as tenant thereof.

The Dwelling-house contains the Old Dining Hall, in which George Fox's meetings were held, a Parlour, formerly the study of George Fox, a large and commodious Kitchen, Scullery, three spacious Bedrooms panelled with Oak, a large Attic and Cellar, and the usual outbuildings and conveniences.

The Buildings include Stable, Byres, Coach House, Barn, Granary, Piggeries, and other outhouses.

The following is a Schedule of this Lot:—

No. on Ordnance Map, 2nd Edition.	Name.	Quantity. A.	R.	P.
629	Swarthmoor Hall, Buildings, &c.	1	1	18
Part 620	Low Bridge Meadow	4	2	31
621	Low Bridge Wood	0	2	1
622	Great Boushay	10	1	5
623	Little Boushay	2	3	37
626	Great Dragley or Barley Field	9	2	3
627	Bull Copy	4	0	37
628	Parrock	0	2	6
630	Wood	1	1	21
631	Orchard	1	2	12
632	Lime Kiln Gill	0	1	34
633	Calf Parrock	2	0	14
634	Lime Kiln Field	12	0	1
635	Lime Kiln Gill	0	1	14
Part 636	Swarthmoor Hall Wood	0	2	1
637	Do.	3	1	32
Part 527	High Meadow	1	2	18
Part 571	Low Bridge Wood	0	0	12
573	Little Dragley or Little Barley Field	3	3	17
574	Old Wife Close	9	1	27
575	Low Meadow	6	0	88
	TOTAL	77	0	17

The property is favourably situated within a few minutes walk from Ulverston Station. The land is highly productive, well watered, and in an excellent state of cultivation.

EXCURSUS IX

THE THIRTEEN SELECTED FRIENDS 1912

William Hanbury Aggs 1870-1953 40 in 1911 barrister at law of 13 Ladbroke Terrace London Probate £24858/11/5

He wrote *The Law of Property 1925*

He was the son of Thomas Aggs and his wife Ann Christy Hanbury. His Great-grandmother Aggs was a Gurney of the Quaker banking family. His uncles was Sir Thomas Hanbury and his cousin Sir Cecil Hambury MP. He married Sylvia daughter Professor Sylvanus Thompson. Her sister Alice Irene Thompson married Thomas Edmund Harvey MP another member of the Selected Friends

His grandmother was a Gibbins and through her he was a cousin of William Waterhouse Gibbins another of the selected friend

Edward Backhouse 1877-?/ 34 in 1911 [?descendent Yealand family] local director of family bank of Whitehouse Stockton on Tees. He was the son of James Edward Backhouse and his wife Edward Barclay Fowler. His great-grandparents were Jonathan Backhouse and his wife Ann Pease. The Backhouse baronets are also descended from Jonathan and Ann. Edward married his second cousin Lucy Backhouse Mounsey. Her sister Amelia Elizabeth married Anthony Wallis another of the selected Friends

Alfred Brooks 1861-1952 ? 49 in 1911 cement manufacturer married children of Hillside London Rd Grays Essex Probate over £5000

He was born at Gravesend son of Edmund Wright Brooks from Melksham and his wife Lucy Ann Marsh. His grandson Anthony Brooks gained the MC and the DSO

Edward Cadbury 1873- 1948 38 in 1911 managing director cocoa and chocolate manufacturer married children of West Holme, Oak Tree Lane, Kings Norton, Selly Oak Probate £380485/13/7

Son of George Cadbury and his wife Mary Tyler married Dorothy Hewitt

He was a cousin of William Waterhouse Gibbins another of the select friends

Roger Clark 1871-1961 39 in 1911 shoe manufacturer married 2 sons 1 dau of Street Soomerset Probate £12445/-/6

Son of William Stephens Clark by his wife Helen Priestman Bright. She was a daughter of John Bright MP. Clark married Sarah Bancroft and their son William Bancroft Clark married a daughter of Field Marshall Smuts

William Waterhouse Gibbins 1869-1953 42 in 1911 director Birmingham battery and metal Co Ltd at Grand Hotel Birminmgham on census night with wife but of Gloucester Probate £90600/8/4. Son of William Cadbury Gibbins by his wife Phoebe Waterhouse. His grandmother was a Cadbury of the same family as Edward Cadbury another of the select friends. On his mothers side he was a cousin of Alfred Waterhouse the architect and to Lord Bridges. He was also kin to William Hanbury Aggs

Wilfred Grace 1873-1920 38 in 1911 chartered accountant married 2 children of 9 Redland Green Bristol Probate £11337/2/4

He was the son of Henry Grace and Hannah Mary Neave He was descended from the Thomas Abraham who went bankrupt in 1753

Thomas Edmund Harvey MP 1874-1955 36 in 1911 retd civil servant unmarried of The Grove Roundhay Leeds Probate over £5000

He was the son of William Harvey by his wife Anna Maria Whiting. He married Alice Irene Thompson whose sister Sylvia married William Hanbury Aggs

He was the warden of Swarthmoor Settlement in Leeds and also of Toynbee Hall

Alfred John King born ca 1862 Monmouth son of William King and his wife Elizabeth Mary Webb. He was a political secretary of 34 Beaufort Rd Birmingham. He Married Ruth Edith Adams and had a daughter Ruth

George B(raithwaite) Lloyd 1886-?? 25 in 1911 wrought iron tube manufacturer single of Edgbaston Grove Birmingham (22 room house with 7 servants)

James Doyle Penrose 38 in 1901 sculptor, artist painter of Finchley Rd St Johns Wood Probate £26239/-/5

Son of James Doyle Pernrose and his wife Annie Bowles b Dublin 1862 married Elizabeth Peckover had three sons Lionel, Sir Roland and Bernard. Lionel in turn was father of Oliver a Mathematics professor, Sir Roger Penrose mathematician inventor of a regular non repeating pattern and a professor and Jonathan Penrose chessmaster

Alfred Leopold Reckitt 1878 -1947 33 in 1911 managing director of starch, blue, black lead and metal polish manufacturer single of 20 Dulwich Wood Park, Norwood, London Probate £549854/-/8. He was born in Hull the son of George Reckitt and his wife Elizabeth Sarah Jackson. His father's sister Elizabeth married Henry Wallis and was grandmother of Anthony Wallis another of the select friends

Ernest William Rowntree C B E 1878-1936 b Scarbrough 33 in 1911 civil servant in lodgings later senior civil servant Probate £7924/7/11. The Rowntrees derive from the Yorkshire Coast, One branch stayed in Scarbrough and made furniture the other branch moved to York and made chocolate. Ernest William belonged to the Scarbrough branch. He was the son of William Stickney Rowntree draper and upholsterer and his wife Anna Mary Doncaster

Allan Tangye 1871-1950 40 in 1911 solicitor married four children of Fair Oaks Farquaher Rd, Edgbaston house with 15 rooms 5 servants Probate £ 73507 /18/3

He was the son of George Tangye by his wife Mary Catherine Weston. His father George together with his brother Richard had offered £5000 for Birmingham City Art Gallery

Anthony Wallis 1880-1919 31 in 1911 H M Inspector with Board of Education married 1 son Probate £9772/3/1 He was the son of Henry Marriage Wallis and his wife Sarah Elizabeth Crossfield his grandmother was aunt to Alfred Leopold Reckitt. He Married Amelia Elizabeth Mounsey daughter of Edmund Backhouse Mounsey and sister of Edward Backhouse. His mother's father was Joseph Crosfield and his niece was the Phoebe Waterhouse who was the mother William Waterhouse Gibbins

Of the thirteen only Wilfred Grace was as far as I know related to Emma Clark Abraham being a fellow descendent of Daniel Abraham and Rachel Fell. But seven of them were in various ways related to each other Aggs, Backhouse, Cadbury, Gibbins, Harvey, Reckitt and Wallis. A composite pedigree would look rather like a London Tube Map. This may only reflect the fact that the Quakers were a fairly small religious group and made a practice of marrying fellow Quakers. The group sufficiently prosperous to participate would be even smaller. I have included probate figures of their financial circumstances.

EXCURSUS X

THE FARMERS

A farmer called Park abandoned his tenancy in the 1920s because of the poor quality of the ground. William Burch was there by 1926 dying in 1932 to be followed by Frederick Burch. Frederick's daughter Mrs Mary Martin wrote a book about her experiences growing up at Swarthmoor Hall called *"Childhood days at Swarthmoor Hall - Growing up in a Quaker manor house"* The Burch's lived in what has been referred to as the cottage, which the Abraham family lived in the rest of the hall. However a relative of William Burch tells me that he and his family lived in one of the houses attached to the Long Barn. These farmers farmed the Hall's home farm. Later a new farm house half a mile down the road to Swarthmoor Village was built. The farmer is a Mr Morphet

Alfred Burch was leasing Hazlehead at Swarthmoor in 1899 from John Ashburner.

CONCLUSION

George Fell the elder remains somewhat unknown, when he first appears in the record he is living in Ulverston, He is buying and selling property both on his own account and as agent for other people. I think that is what is meant by the term attorney in his case. He seems to have been successful and became relatively wealthy. He was offered a knighthood and was able to send his son to Oxford and to Gray's Inn as many local gentry did. His origins are obscure though almost certainly local to Furness. He could have been Ulverston born or moved in from Pennington, Dalton, Urswick or any of the surrounding villages.

His son Thomas continued the family's rise to affluence. He was involved by his father in the business of buying and selling land and property, which he seems to have continued in tandem with his legal and political affairs. He amassed a large landed estate and was involved in various commercial activities. He owned three water corn mills in Ulverston and three more with a windmill in Dalton.. He had a successful legal career and was thought to be a just judge. He did well out of the civil war and parliamentary period. He was a puritan and remained a member of the Church of England. We have his wife's testimony for that. He tolerated and protected the Quakers allowing them to meet in his house. This is more remarkable in that he did not live in an age that regarded tolerance as a virtue. He was happily married to his wife Margaret. They had nine children of which eight grew to maturity. They were fortunate in that circumstance, Medical science was only just beginning and had little effect on one's chances of survival after acquiring an infection. He died in his late fifties

Much has been written about Margaret. She was a formidable woman, not afraid to go and petition the king in person, or the parliamentary leaders either. She had a forceful personality and would have dominated her children's lives if they had not been as strong minded as she was herself.

George Fell younger has had a bad press. He was very fond of his father. He too was a lawyer and he too was a member of the Church of England. He took the royalist side at the restoration and this helped him to preserve the family's fortune which might otherwise have been confiscated. He was not a Quaker and this did not please his mother. He did not approve of her marrying again. In his will he does not mention his mother and at one point refers to his sisters as the daughters of his father. He too died young leaving a widow and two small children other children having died in childhood.

Hannah Fell who was George's wife and widow came from London commercial and legal circles with Presbyterian and royalist sympathies. Her first husband had got entangled in an abortive plot to bring about the restoration of the monarchy. She also was a strong character waging intermittent war with her mother in law and doing everything possible to protect her children's rights. Her brother in law Richard Tomlinson evidently thought she was trustworthy. She and indeed George were involved in disputes over property in London deriving from her first husband and her first husband's first wife.

Charles Fell transferred his life to the London area and sold his rights to Swarthmoor to Daniel Abraham. His son also Charles married a granddaughter of William Penn and with her acquired a fortune as the Penn family seemed to own vast acres of land in Pennsylvania.

Judge Fell's daughters; Margaret married John Rouse merchant of London and Barbados; They had a number of children. Bridget married John Draper of Headlam Durham and died shortly afterwards having had two children who both died young. I find no evidence to support the suggestion of one author that she had mental health problems like her Aunt Frances Richardson: Isabel married twice firstly to William Yeomans by whom she had with other children who died young a son William who lived at Swarthmoor Hall but died at 22. Isabel subsequently married Abraham Morrice a mercer from Lincoln. She must have got on well with her brother George because she and her issue are next in his will if his own children did not survive to maturity and his surviving daughter shared her name., Sarah kept the accounts after her father's death and her account book is a treasure of information about the economy of the estate. She married William Mead a merchant of the City of London their son Nathaniel was sergeant at law and was knighted: Mary married Thomas Lower a physician and a widower originally from Cornwall and brother of Richard Lower physician to Charles II. They eventually settled at Marsh Grange and had many children,: Susanna married William Ingram: Rachel stayed at home and married Daniel Abraham and they shared imprisonment with Margaret Fell,.

Daniel Abraham was a man of tender conscience. The worst of the persecution would be over by the time he took over the hall in 1691. The toleration Acts allowed them to meet for worship. He got fined and so on for refusing to pay tithes because they went to the upkeep of the steeple house clergy. Evidently George Fox had thought clergy should not be paid. He was the son of John Abraham a successful Manchester businessman and a Quaker. His religious beliefs did cost him money but he survived.

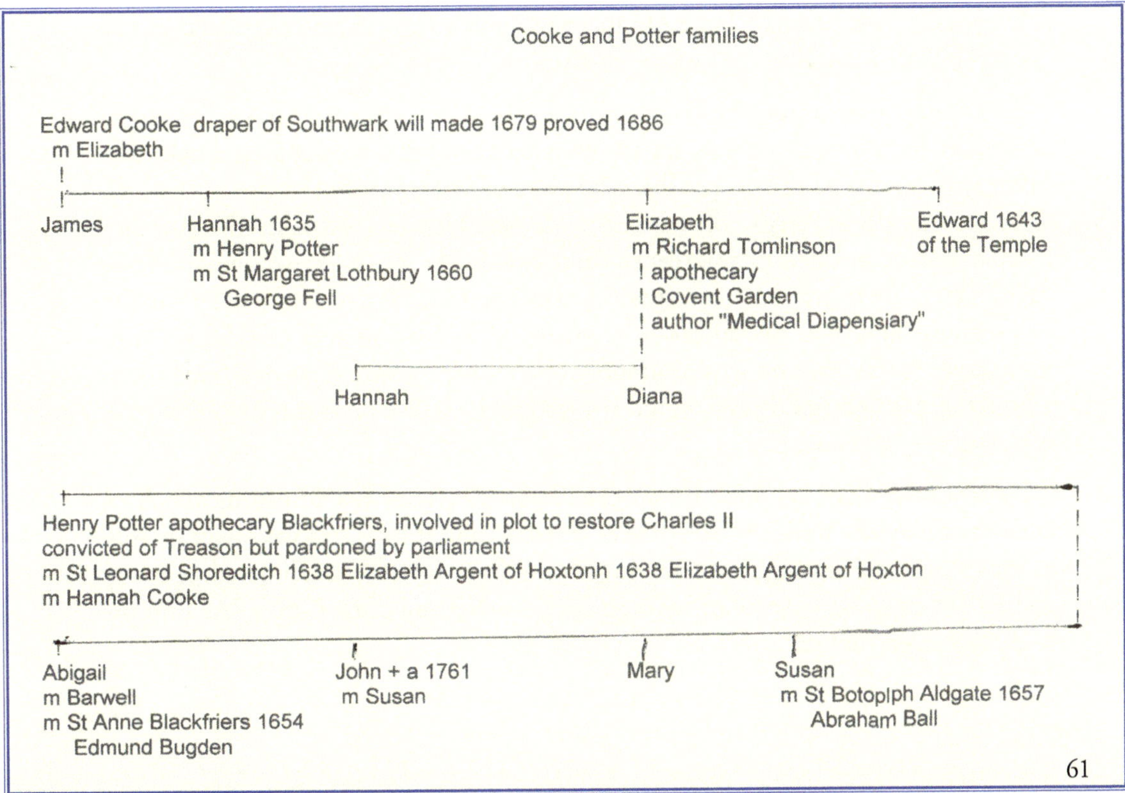

His son John Abraham known as "Lord Abraham" presumably because he was lord of the manor seems to spent a lot of time selling or mortgaging land. He married an heiress Sarah Foster. Towards the end of his management he had drawn up a list of lands he was willing to sell and those he wished to keep. He did try to sell to fellow Quakers. He handed his estate over to his son Thomas

Thomas Abraham was a grocer and merchant in Whitehaven. He was either very unlucky or had poor judgement. At times he sailed close to the wind it looks as though he mortgaged the same piece of property to different people at the same time. Unsurprisingly he went bankrupt.

Thomas Petty stepped in buying everything up and settling all the creditors. He then sold the estate to James Jackson a hatter of Ulverston brother in law and business associate of William Lindow, to whom he transferred the estate in 1763

William Lindow was a mariner, a ship's captain, engaged in the slave trade. He started as agent for Rawlinsons of Lancaster in Grenada. He was prominent in Grenada and very successful. He retired to Lancaster and married Abigail Rawlinson. He was a competent business man engaged in a regrettable industry.

Neither of his successors lived at the property though William Lindow Dickinson took an interest in the cattle farmed their. They had a succession of tenants and tenant farmers. The best known tenant was Fr William West who wrote "The Antiquities of Furness"

Eventually Miss Emma Clarke Abraham was able to buy the property and in due course it came into the hands of the Society of Friends

Even today Swarthmoor Hall is surrounded by fields. One field does show signs of former buildings but these are thought to have been for lodging stock. The mystery is where did the people live who were of Swarthmoor but not of the hall. One possibility is at Petty Croft where the Meeting House now stands. Swarthmoor is separately mentioned in a sixteenth century subsidy roll with two taxpayers one called Petty, There are some cottages near the Meeting House which is on the site of previous buildings. Swarthmoor originally would be an area of land without necessarily any houses on it. Presumably of the two George Fells of Swarthmoor who refused knighthoods one would live where the hall is now and the other elsewhere in the larger area.

I suspect the financial difficulties of the later Abrahams would not have helped them maintain the building to a proper standard and if the Lindows saw it mainly as an income generating device it might well have become dilapidated as many testify, but there is evidence of maintenance work being done during the Lindow and Dickinson period.

APPENDIX A

WILL OF GEORGE FELL SNR

George x Fell the elder of Swarthmoor copy made 1681 LA WRW/F

I George Fell of Swarthmoor the older, sick in body, but perfect in mind and memory, praised be God, do make and ordain this my last will and testament in manner and form following

My Soul I bequeath into the hand of my Blessed Lord and Saviour Jesus Christ hoping to be saved by his precious death and passion, and my body to be buried in the Parish Church at Ulverston.

Item, I do hereby revoke and make void all former wills and testaments made by me and concerning my personal estate I do dispose of it in the manner following

Item I do give unto Frances Corker daughter of Thomas Corker and my grandchild £1/6/8 yearly for seven years next after my decease to be paid by my son Thomas Fell forth of the close I bought of Reginald Holme and the close I bought of Francis Corker and the dale I bought of Myles Hunter, to be paid as he thinks for bringing her up.

Item I give unto Jennett Corker daughter of the said Thomas Corker and my grandchild five pounds due forth of Hawkswell Rent at Candlemass 1638 and to be paid by my son Thomas Fell and my son in law Henry Lindow for four years next after my decease and to employ it only for her.

Item, it is my will and mind that whereas Robert Gaitskell stands bound unto me in the sum of £80 by bond upon condition to pay £40 to me if my grandchild Margaret Gaitskell do die not leaving sons or before she comes to years, according to the condition of the said bond, then it is my mind that my son Thomas Fell shall have £10 forth of the said forty pounds, and my daughter Alice £7/10/- and Thomas Corker's children £7/10/- and Henry Lindow of Scathwaitte's children £7/10/- and the last £7/10/- residue of the said forty pounds to Thomas Cooper's children to be put forth at the discretion of my son Thomas Fell

Further it is my will and mind that my son Thomas Fell shall keep my daughter Alice till she comes to ye aforesaid age twenty years and that he shall have use of her portion £8 yearly for finding her meat, drink, apparel and lodging and the residue to be put forth for her use till she comes to the age aforesaid. It is also my will and mind that if my daughter Alice Fell do marry without the private liking and consent of my son Thomas Fell, that then she shall have but £100 and the remainder the one half to my son Thomas Fell and his children, and the other half to be divided equally amongst the rest of grandchildren. It is likewise my will and mind that if my daughter Alice Fell shall die & depart this natural life before she come to the age of 18 years or marriage that then one half of her portion to go to the use of my son Thomas Fell, and £10 of the other half of her portion to be paid to my son in law Thomas Gateskell's daughter, if it pleases God she live, and twenty marks to be divided equally amongst Henry Ofley's children and the remainder of the other half to be equally divided among Thomas Corker's children, Thomas Cooper's children and Henry Lindow's children.

Item I give unto Margaret Gatskell my grandchild £11 to be paid but to her at age 18 years if she be then living

Item, I give unto Alice Holme my servant twenty shillings, to James Pettie 20s, to ye poor of the parish of Ulverston 20s, whereof 10s be given them at May day and 10s at Christmas next after my death

Item I give unto Robert Towerrs 10s

Item I give unto Alice Pettie wife of Myles Pettie 6/8 and to John Pettie 6/8

Item I give James Towers son of William Towers 8/-

Executors of this my last will and testament I nominate and appoint Thomas Fell my son and Alice Fell my daughter

Witnesses Thomas Gateskell Jnr, Thomas Corker Jnr

APPENDIX B
WILL OF THOMAS FELL

PCC will PROB/11/285/145 4th December 1658

The twenty-third day of September in the year of our Lord God One thousand six hundred fifty and eight be it remembered that the day and year before written Thomas Fell of Swarthmoor in the county of Lancaster esquire being sick and weak of body but of a perfect memorie and understanding, blessed be the Lord for the same, doth hereby declare and publish his last will and testament in manner and form following (that is to say) he doth appoint, nominate and ordain Richard Radcliffe yeoman and Thomas Coulton yeoman both my menial servants to be my executors jointly and severally nevertheless upon this trust and confidence and to the end and purpose following (that is to day) after my debts, funeral expenses and legacies discharged then they shall give the residue and overplus of all my real and personal estate to my seven daughters Margarett, Bridgett, Isabell, Sarah, Marie, Susanna and Rachell equally to be divided amongst them. to whom I do give the residue and remainder of all my real and personal estate equally amongst them, my debts, legacies and funeral expenses being first discharged as aforesaid, First I give and bequeath unto the most aged, impotent and necessitous persons within the parish of Ulverston, the sum of ten pounds distributed by my executors taking the information and assistance of the overseers of the poor within the parish. Secondly I give and bequeath to the overseers of the poor of the said parish for the time being thirty pounds with the interest where of they are to put forth or more yearly the poorest children born within the town of Ulverston excluding such as are born in the hamlet or elsewhere, saving only those that are born within the precincts of the said town and the overseers of the poor for the time being shall have the consent and allowance of such person or persons as shall be hereon owners of my estate at Swarthmoor forth putting forth such impotent persons yearly. I likewise give and bequeath thirty pounds for the interest there of yearly is to go towards the maintenance of a schoolmaster to be kept at Ulverstone for the teaching of poor children which sum of thirty pounds are to pay within one year after my decease to such person or persons who will give unto them good security for answering yearly the interest thereof to the end and purpose aforesaid. Item

I give and bequeath five pounds unto the most aged, impotent and necessitous persons within the parish of Dalton to be distributed by my executors taking information and assistance from the overseers of the poor within the said parish. I likewise give and bequeath to my very honourable and noble friend the Lord Bradshaw ten pounds to buy a ring therewith whom I humbly beseech to accept thereof and all the acknowledgement I can make and thankfulness for his ancient and continued kindness undeservedly vouchsafed unto me since first acquaintance. I likewise give unto Mary Askew twenty pounds for her faithful and careful service performed unto my wife and children in all their extremities. I further give and bequeath unto Joseph Sharpe my faithful and careful servant at the Marsh Grange fifty shllings and the like sum unto Anne Jaykes who has approved herself a very honest and careful servant ever since she came to the Marsh. I do hereby likewise give and bequeath unto my dear, careful and entirely beloved wife Margaret Fell fifty pounds a token and testimony of a dearest affection unto her. I likewise give unto James Fell my servant twenty shillings to buy himself a ring as a token of my love unto him. I likewise give unto Thomas Knipe of the manor my old true friend twenty shillings to buy himself a ring therewith, a small token of the remembrance of my love for him. AS for my executors who are to have no other benefit nor advantage by this my will and testament than hereafter expressed (that is to say) I give to each of them five pounds apiece for the pain and care they are to undergo in the discharge and trust hereby imposed on them and concerning they or either of them shall be put to in proving this my will and other necessaries incident thereunto and in recovering or sueing for any debts or defending any suit commenced against them as my executors they same is to be deducted and taken forth out the residue and remainder of my personal estate my debts and legacies being first discharged. I desire my very true friends Anthony Pearson of Rampshawe in the county of Durham and Jarvise Benson of Heaygarth in the county of York gentleman to endeavour what in them lies to that this my last will and testament truly performed by my executors To whom (set) the said Anthony and Jervise I do give forty shillings a piece, desiring them to except of it to buy each of them a ring therewith. I do hereby revoke and make void all former wills and testaments by me made. And I do hearby give unto my beloved son George Fell so many of my law books which will make up those that he hath the complete body of the law And wherein they prove defective my executors shall sell so many of the rest of my law books as will buy those that are wanting. I do hereby in further token of my love and affection to my dear wife give and bequeath unto her my dwelling house onset with all the buildings, stables, barns, orchards gardens therewithal used and occupied with fifty acres of ground lying most conveniently to the said house and to be set out and divided by my executors. All which hereby I give and bequeath unto my said loving wife son long as she will continue and remain remain in my name and as my widow and unmarried to any other and no longer.In hope that she will be careful and loving to my poor fatherless children. And l;astly I do publish, ordain and declare this to be my last will and testament.. In witness whereof I have hereto set my hand and seal the day and year first above written.

Thomas Fell

Witnesses George Fell, Thomas Knype, Thomas Greaves, William Benson

This will was proved at London before the judges of probate of wills and granting administration lawfully authorised the fourth day of December in the year of our Lord one thousand and six hundred and fifty and eight by the oath of Richard Ratcliffe joint executors named in the said will, to whom administration of all and singular of the goods chattels and debts of the said deceased was committed they being first legally sworn to legally administer the same.

APPENDIX C

WILL OF GEORGE FELL JNR

Will George Fell of Swarthmoor

The seventh day of October in the year of our Lord one thousand six hundred and seventy; I George Fell of Swarthmoor, in the County of Lancaster Esquire being of sound and perfect memory though weak and infirm of body, do make this my last will and testament in manner and form following, first I commend my soul into the merciful hands of God, hoping through his mercy and the merit of Christ my saviour for pardon of my sins and salvation, my body I desire may be buried in the parish church of Ulverston as near to my father as with convenience it may, and in such decent manner as by executrix shall think meat. As for my temporal estate, I dispose thereof as follows: (viz) All my messuages, lands, tenements, milnes, manors or lordships and other hereditaments, whatsoever; I give and bequeath unto Charles my son and the heirs of his body, lawfully to be begotten, charges and chargeable as hereafter is expressed, and for default of such issue I give and devise the same unto Isabel my daughter and the heirs of her body lawfully to be begotten charged and chargeable as aforesaid, and for default of such issue I give unto my wife Hannah Fell all my whole estate, so long as she keeps as my wife and my widow, and it it shall happen that Charles shall live to have issue, then he is to pay unto Isabel my daughter, when she shall attain to the age of one and twenty years, or at the day of her marriage, one thousand pounds forth of the money from milnes in Low Furness, and for default of such issue, I give and bequeath unto William Yeoman and his wife and to his wife for ever all the lands and tenements called Haukswell and More house, as also the Manor or Lordship of Blawith, and in default of such issue of my son and daughter; I give and devise unto Thomas Fell of Scathwaite and to the heirs male of his body lawfully begotten, the Manor or Lordship of Ulverston, Swarthmore, Osmotherley with all the lands about Swarthmore, Dragley Beck and the milnes in Ulverston excepting two acres next adjoining to the little house, where Thomas Greaves now dwells; and the said little house which I give to the said Thomas Greaves and his heirs) and all other hereditaments in Ulverstone aforesaid, charged and chargeable as is hereafter expressed, (That is to say) in case the same do for default of issue of my son and daughter fall and come to the said Thomas Fell and his heirs, then and not otherwise, I charge the same with the payment of five hundred pounds; ((of which)) to Edward Cooke of the Temple £200, Mr Hodgkinson £100, Sackville Greaves £100 and to Mr Samuel Richardson £100; and in default of issue male on the body lawfully begotten of the said Thomas Fell ; then I give and bequeath unto Edward Fell of Stockport in the County of Cheshire gentleman and to the heirs male of his body lawfully begotten all the aforesaid manors or lordships of Ulverston, Swarthmore, Dragley Beck and the milnes of Ulverston and all other hereditaments with the appurtenances; and in default of such issue male on the body of Edward Fell; I give and bequeath the aforesaid Manor or Lordship of Ulverston, Swarthmore, Osmotherley and all other hereditaments with the appurtenances, equally to be divided amongst my sisters and their heirs; And I do further charge the Town Milne with the payment of four pounds yearly to be paid to Thomas Coulton during his natural life and I do also charge the said Over Milne in Ulverstone with the payment of three pounds yearly to James Ellithorne during his natural life, which two last mentioned charges shall commence immediately after my decease, and if it happen that my son and daughter shall die without issue then I give and bequeath the aforesaid Town Milne unto Thomas Coulton during his natural life and the said Over Milne unto James Ellithorne during his natural life; also in default of issue of my son and daughter as aforesaid and the death of my wife or her marriage, I give all my four milnes situate within the parish of Dalton to my sisters, daughters of my father and their heirs equally to be divided amongst them; Also whereas already by my deed poll bearing date the thirtyfirst day of August last granted unto Sackville Greaves esquire and his heirs all those my messuages, tenements and hereditaments called Marsh Grange within the Manor of Furness which deed was made in trust to the said Sackville Greaves; that he and his heirs after my decease should sell the tenements thereby granted for the payment of my debts and the overplus of the money raised thereby (if any be) to be paid to my Executrix for the use of my said daughter and the bettering of her portion, to which purpose I have made a declaration by an indenture under my hand and seal : Now I do will and devise that the same trust shall be performed accordingly and the premises I do appoint to be sold, with what conveniency may; and the money thence arising I appoint for payment of my just debts and the overplus (if any be) for my daughter; and if the price fall short of the payment of my debts, I appoint what is wanting shall be paid out of my personal estate, or any other estate that I have and that care be taken that no person engaged with me do suffer

Also I do give unto my loving wife the portions of my son and daughter during their minorities and of their portions and rights until the respectively attain the age of one and twenty years, if she so long continue my widow, recommending to her the care of their education; and if she die or marry before that time, then I desire and appoint for their tutors the said Sackville Greaves and Edward Cook my father-in-law. Also I give unto my Uncle Matthew Richardson and to Mr George Hillton four pounds apiece to buy each a ring, hoping for their assistance to my wife and children. Also I give unto Mary Caton twenty pounds, also I give unto Sackville Greaves forty pounds to buy him a ring, Also I give unto Mr Edward Cooke my father-in-law and to Mrs Elizabeth Cooke my mother in law; Mr Edward Cooke of the Temple, Mr Richard Tomlinson an apothecary in Covent Garden and to Elizabeth his wife forty shillings apiece to buy them rings. Also I give unto Mr Thomas Hodgkinson my best horse, my best gun and my best case of pistols, Also I give and bequeath unto the most aged, impotent and necessitous person in the parish of Ulverston ten pounds. Also I give and bequeath unto the most aged and necessitous persons in the parish of Dalton five pounds; also I give and bequeath to every servant of my house twenty shillings a piece and to Thomas Greaves forty shillings

Executrix of this my will I make my loving wife to whom I give all the rest of my goods & personal estate, my debts, legacies and funeral discharged; declaring that it is not my meaning by any devise of lands or tenements with in this will to deebarr her of her dower or widow right therein

In witness I have hereunto set my hand and seal the day and year first above written

Witnesses Thomas Richardson, Henry Kidson, Mary Caton, Thomas Coulton

Note by A C A The above was copied from a copy (no doubt contemporary) which was among the old letters and papers of Miss Ellen Grace (+1907) who got them from Mrs Mary Thirnbeck, to whom they were given by her mother (Sarah Abraham) It (the original copy) was no doubt made either for Margaret Fell (his mother) or her daughters

ACA presumably Alfred Clay Abraham a brother of Emma Clark Abraham

However there are differences between this copy at Friends House and the following one at Lancaster Archives most notably that Edward Fell is of Stopyard in Cheshire wherever that may be.

Furness Will WRW F

The second day of October in the year of our Lord one thousand six hundred and seventy I George Fell of Swarthmoor in the County of Lancaster Esquire being of sound and perfect memory though weak and infirm of body do make this my last will and testament in manner and form late present. First I commend my soul unto the merciful hands of God hoping through his mercie and the merits of Christ my Saviour for pardon of my sins and salvarew my bodie ....pen be buried in the parish Church of Ulverston as near to my father as with convenience it may and in such decent manner as my executrix shall think meet. As for my temporal .... I grant thereof as follows (viz) All my messuages, lands, tenements, mills Manors or lordships and other hereditaments whatsoever, I give and bequeath to Charles my son and the issue of his body lawfully to be begotten charged and chargeable as hereafter is written. And for default of such issue I give and demise the same to Isabel my daughter and the issue of her body lawfully to be begotten charged and chargeable as aforesaid. And for default of such issue I give unto my wife Hannah Fell for as long as she keeps as my wife and my widow. And if shall happen that Charles shall live to have issue then he is to pay unto Isabel my daughter when she shall attain the age of one and twenty or at the day of her marriage one thousand pounds forth of the mills in Low Furness. And for default of such issue I give and bequeath to William Yeomans and his wife and to their heirs for ever all the lands and tenements called Hawkeswell and Morehouse and also the manor or lordship of Blawith. And in default of such issue of my son and daughter I give and demise unto Thomas Fell of Scathwaite and to the heirs male of his body lawfully begotten the manor and lordship of Ulverston, Swarthmoor and Osmotherley with all the lands about Swarthmoor and Dragley Beck and the mills in Ulverston excepting two acres next adjoining the little house where Thomas Greaves now dwells and the said little house which I give to the said Thomas Greaves and his heirs; and all other houses lands inUlverston aforesaid charged and chargeable as is hereafter expressed, that is to say in case the same do for default of issue of my son and daughter and all come to the said Thomas Fell and his heirs then and not otherwise I charge the same with the payment of the sum of five hundred pounds. To Edmund Cooke of the Temple two hundred pounds, Mr Hodgkinson one hundred pounds, Sackville Greaves one hundred pounds and to Mr Samuel Richardson one hundred pounds. And in default of issue male of issue male of the body of the said Thomas Fell lawfully begotten then I give and bequeath unto Edward Fell of Stopyard in the County of Cheshire gentleman and to the heirs of his body lawfully begotten all the aforesaid manor and Lordship of Ulverston, Swarthmoor Dragley Beck and the mills at Ulverston and all other hereditaments with their appurtenances. And in default of such issue male of the body of Edward Fell, I give and bequeath the aforesaid manor and lordship of Ulverston, Swarthmoor and Osmotherley and all other hereditaments with their appurtenances equally to be divided amongst my sisters and their heirs. And I do further charge the Town Mill with the payment of four pounds yearly to be paid to Thomas Coulton during his natural life. And I do also charge the said Over Mill in Ulverston with the payment of three pounds yearly to James Ellythorne during his natural life which two last mentioned charges of four and three pounds yearly, my will and mind is shall commence immediately after my decease. And if it shall happen that my son and daughter shall die without issue then I give and bequeath the aforesaid Town Milne unto Thomas Coulton during his natural life and the said Over Milne unto James Ellythorne during his natural life. Also in default of issue of my son and daughter as aforesaid and the death of my wife or her marriage I give and bequeath all my four milnes situate in the parish of Dalton to my sisters, daughters of my father and their heirs equally to be divided amongst them.

Also whereas I have already by my deed poll bearing date the thirty first day of August last granted unto Sackville Greaves esquire his heirs all those my messuages, tenements and hereditaments called Marsh Grange within the manor of Furness which deed was made in trust to the said Sackville Greaves.that he and his heirs after my decease should sell the tenements thereby mentioned for the payment of my debts and the overplus of the money raised or sace there of (if any be) to be paid to my executrix for the use of my said daughter and the both my ….. I suppose I have [hole] …declaration of my indenture under my hand and seal. Now I do will and devise that the same trust shall be performed accordingly and the premises I do appoint to sold with what is convenient may [hole] money thence arising I appoint for the payment of my just debts and the surplus (if any be) for my daughter. And if the price fall short of the payment of my debts I appoint that that which is wanting shall be poaid out of my personal estates and other estates that I have and that care be taken that no person engaged with me as surety do suffer thereby. Also I do give unto my loving wife for the education of my son and daughter during their minorities of their possessions and rights until they respectively attain the age of one and twenty years if she so long continues my widow recommending the care of their education. And if she marry or die before that time then I desire and appoint for their tutors the said Sackville Greaves and Edward Cooke my father-in-law. Also I give unto my uncle Matthew Richardson and to Mr George Hilton ten pounds a piece to buy each of them a ring hoping for their assistance to my wife and children. Also I give to Mary Caton twenty pounds.And also I give unto Sackville Greaves forty pounds to buy him a ring Also I give unto Mr Edward Cooke my father-in-law and to Mrs Elizabeth Cooke my mother in law his wife, Mr Edward Cooke of the Temple Mr Richard Tomlinson apothecary in Coven Garden and to Elizabeth his wife each of then forty shillings a piece to buy them a ring I give unto Mr Thomas Hodgkinson my best [hole] my best gun and my best case of pistols. Also I give and bequeath to the most aged and impotent necessitous persons within the parish of Ulverston ten pounds Also I give and bequeath [hole] unto the most aged and necessitous persons within the parish of Dalton five pounds Also I give and bequeath unto every servant at my decease twenty shillings a piece and to [hole] forty shillings. Executrix of this my will I make my said loving wife to whom I give all the rest of my personal estate, my debts, legacies aforesaid [hole] declaring that it is not my meaning by any devise of lands or tenements within this my will to debar her of her dower widow right therin.In witness I hereunto set my hand and seale the day and year first above written

[hole] declared to be my last will and testament in presence of Thomas Richardson, Henry Kidson Mary Caton Thomas Cooulton

Adm by Hannah Fell

APPENDIX D

NOTES ON WILL OF MARGARET FOX

LA WRW/F 3 10 1702

I Margaret x Fox, of Swarthmore in the County of Lancaster widow, being in the eighty fourth year in my age, yet blessed be God, in a good measure of health and of a sound and perfect memory, do make my last will and testament in manner and form following:

First Item I do give unto my son in law Daniel Abraham of Swarthmoor aforesaid and, Joseph Goad of Beakcliffe in the aforesaid County of Lancaster yeoman ten pounds for the poor of the people called Quakers belonging to Swarthmore Meeting to be kept by the said meeting as a stock and the interest of it yearly to help to maintain such poor of the people called Quakers as shall be in want, belonging to Swarthmore Meeting aforesaid

Item I do give to my grandchildren :- Nathaniel Rous, Bethia English, Ann Rous, Nathaniel Meade, Margery Lower, Loveday Lower, Robert Lower, John Lower, Bridget Lower, John Abraham 2 guineas each

Item I do give to my grandchildren Charles Fell, Isabell Greaves & Margaret Manwaring one guinea each

All the remainder and residue of my worldly estate whatsoever I do give to my dear and loving daughter Rachel Abraham wife of Daniel Abraham aforesaid, who hath lived with me many years in my old age and hath diligently and dutifully demeaned herself to me with a great deal of care and tenderness, and I do make my said daughter sole executrix of this my last will and testament, Hereby revoking all other wills and testaments whatsoever formerly made by me.

In witness I have set my hand and seal the sixth day of April Anno Domini one thousand six hundred and ninety eight MF her mark

witness Henry Phillips, William Davis, William Mead, Sarah Read

Proved at Richmond 3rd October 1702

APPENDIX E

THE TRIPARTITE AGREEMENT OF 1691

In which Daniel Abraham buys most of the Swarthmoor Hall Estate from the rest of the Fell Family. This document is at Friends House.

Indenture tripartite made the eight day of July in the this year of our sovereign lord and lady William and Mary majesties of England Scotland France and Ireland King and Queen and defender of the faith anno domini one thousand six hundred and ninety one **Between** Charles Fell of Swarthmoor in the parish of Ulverston in the County of Lancaster son and heir of George Fell late of Marsh Grange in the said County of Lancaster esquire deceased and Mary now wife of the said Charles Fell, Margaret Fox of Swarthmoor widow aforesaid grandmother of the said Charles and heretofore the wife of Thomas Fell late of Swarthmoor aforesaid esquire deceased grandfather of the said Charles Fell, Hannah Fell of Swarthmoor aforesaid widow and relict of the said George Fell and mother of the said Charles Fell, James Greaves of Firlenithe in the County of Sussex esquire and Isabella his wife the only daughter of the said George Fell, John Rous of Kingston upon Thames in the County of Surrey merchant and Margaret his wife, Abraham Morrice of the City of London mercer and Isabella his wife, William Mead of Fannchurch St in the City of London merchant and Sarah his wife, Thomas Lower of Marsh Grange aforesaid within the County of Lancaster gentleman and Mary his wife, William Ingram of the City of London aforesaid tallow chandler and Susanna his wife, Daniel Abraham of Swarthmoor aforesaid gentleman and Rachel his wife, They the said Margaret, Isabella, Sarah, Mary, Susannah and Rachel last mentioned being six of the surviving daughters of the said Thomas Fell and Thomas Colton of Ulverston aforesaid within the said County of Lancaster yeoman and Mary his wife, the said Thomas Colton being the surviving executor of the last will and testament of the said Thomas Fell of the first part, Thomas Richardson of Rownhead in the said County of Lancaster esquire and John Corker of Lund in Ulverston aforesaid gentleman of the second part, and Richard Rawlinson of Dalton-in-Furness in the County of Lancaster aforesaid gentleman and Thomas Richardson of

Whinfield in Furness aforesaid gentleman of the third part **Witnesseth** that the said Charles Fell and Mary his wife in consideration of the sum of three thousand and nine hundred pounds of lawful money of England to him the said Charles Fell in hand paid and secured to them by the said Daniel Abraham pursuant to certain articles of agreement dated the seventh day of March last year and made between us the said Charles Fell and Hannah Fell of the one part and the said Daniel Abraham of the other part in such manner as in and by the said articles is directed at and before the ensealing and delivery of these presents. And the said John Rous Margaret his wife, Abraham Morrice Isabella his wife, William Mead and Sarah his wife, Thomas Lower and Mary his wife, William Ingram Susannah his wife, Daniel Abraham & Rachel his wife in consideration of the respective sums of one hundred pounds a piece of the lawful money severally in hand paid or secured to be paid to them the said John Rous, Abraham Morrice, William Mead, Thomas Lower and William Ingram by the said Daniel Abraham before the execution hereof amounting in the whole to the sum of four thousand pounds five hundred and the sum of five shillings a piece paid to the said Margaret Fox, Hannah Fell, James Greaves and Isabella his wife and Thomas Colton and Mary his wife the receipt of which said several sums as respectively paid them in manner as aforesaid. Then the said Charles Fell, John Rous, Abraham Morrice, William Mead, Thomas Lower, William Ingram, Margaret Fox, Hannah Fell, James Greaves and Thomas Colton do hereby respectively acknowledge and thereof and every part and parcel there of have do severally acquit release and discharge the said Daniel Abraham his heirs executors and administrators by these presents and each and everyone of them hath bargained granted sold alienated suffered ratified and confirmed and by these presents do and any of them do grant bargain sell alienate dispose devised released ratified and confirmed unto the said Richard Rawlinson and Thomas Richardson of Whinfield and their heirs. All those the mannors or lordships or and reputed Mannors or Lordships of Ulverston and Blawith in the said County of Lancaster. And the court leet and view of Frank Pledge and all to court leet or view of frank pledge belonging within the same manor of lordships of Ulverston and Blawith pn said county of Lancaster or which hereafter may or ought to belong thereunto together with all and singular the Royalties, franchises, rents, fines, town terms greatfines renthens, boones duties and services as well of the free as of the copyhold or customary tenants, lands tenements hereditaments profits rights members and appurtenances whatsoever to the said mannors or lordships of Ulverston and Blawith or either of them or any part or parcel thereof respectively belonging or in any wise appertaining or accepted reputed taken or known to be part and parcel member there or of any part thereof respectively And all that capital messuage or mansion house with all its Aishto members and appurtenances heretofore commonly called and known by the name of Swarpemoor als Swarthmoor and now called and commonly known by the name of Swarthmoor Hall situate standing and being in the parish of Ulverston in the said County of Lancaster, And all and singular the several messuages closes inclosures and parcels of arable moor and pasture ground herein hereafter particularly named with their and every of their rights members and appurtenances lying and being within Ulverston, Swarthmoor, Dragleybecks, Urswick and Pennington in the said County of Lancaster or any of them to the said capital messuage or Mansion House belonging or appertaining or therein shall now or heretofor occupied as demesnes or demesne lands or otherwise that is to say the Great Levyheads and Harpinshaw, the Gillclose and...The Oldwife close and Staney and staneyend close therein the Coppy the Great Close and Dragley Dicky Croft the Gutterlands Holmes als the Holmes the Gutterlands Henry Benson's fields with the dwelling house, barnes, stables, outhouses and other buildings and the hempgarth and parroke with the appurtenances now in the possession or occupation of Thomas Greaves and Samuel Greaves his son or their assigns which is adjoining to the said Henry Benson's field the Sowre, Bowshaw the Highbridge meadows the Broaddale Diccon Dale the dale at Barnbeck containing by estimation three acres or thereabouts be they more or less the Greediford meadow, Greediford close, Longslackdale, Dodgson wife close, Reginald Holme close with the grounds now therein heretofor called Kate close, Aingsley the Great dales als the Broadaless, the Little dales als the Langdales the Little Levyheads and woods, Pettygill als Gillwood & Cowclose als the Lund Meadow the Starmeadow Lundroyd meadow, the Whitewell meadow, the Greatcoate lands the Little [ ] Steele close and Clough, Pette, the West end, Westend Fields the Great Woody acres the two Little woody acres the Lothdales with the houses and barn thereon standing, Greatcroft Addison close New Close Stonedens Common Parrock the Adwife house and onset with the outhouses thereof and the closes thereto adjoining commonly call Oldwife House als Kirby Close, Trinkeld field als Longdale Genite acre, the Wellnook Wellhead Croft by estimation half an acre (be it more or less) Rattenrow Croft als Seggerston Acre, Tarn Bank Close and the two Flan Closes which said closes and parcels of ground herein before last named do contain in the whole by estimation one hundred and eighty acres or thereabouts (be it more or less) and all other the lands, grounds, hereditaments, whatsoever to the said capital messuage or mansion house belonging or in anywise of right appertaining or therewith now or heretofore used by occupied or enjoyed as demesne or demesne lands or otherwise or accepted reputed occupied used demised taken or known to be as part parcel or mentioned thereof or as belonging thereto with their and every of their appurtenances And also all that house the messuage, tenement, lands grounds with all those rights, members and appurtenances commonly known by the name of Hawxwell als Hawkswell situate and lying in the parish of Ulverston aforesaid within the said County of Lancaster heretofore in the several tenures and possessions of George Fell deceased great grandfather, the said Thomas Fell the grandfather, the said George Fell the father of the said Charles Fell or some of them or some of their assigns and now in tenure and passion of said Charles Fell and Hannah Fell or one of them their or one of their assigns, with all arable meadows pasture grazing thereunto belonging with appurtenances containing by estimation fourscore acres of ground or thereabouts be the same more or less and also all the sheepheave or pasturage for the sheep and cattle upon the moor and commons thereunto belonging with appurtenances and all and every of the lands grounds moore, mossy commons, common of pasture and turbary privileges and hereditaments belonging to the same messuage, tenement lands and premises called Hawkswell belonging and or otherwise appertaining or to or with the same or any parcel now or therebefore at any time used, occupied demised or enjoyed or accepted reputed had or taken as part parcel or member thereof with their rights members or appurtenances and all those rents of assize with the said manot lordship of Ulverston ((start of second membrane)) Of Ulverston issueing out of diverse free burgages lands and hereditaments their payable at the feast of St Martin in Winter only by the particular there of amounting to thirty shillings and four pence by the year or thereabouts be the same more or less. And also all that free rent of fifteen shillings heretofore payable by Henry Marquess of Dorset for lands and hereditaments in Ulverston aforesaid And also all that free rents of diverse tenants for certain sums and [] of dower and the fee farm for his part of Ulverston payable yearly at the same feast of St Martin. shillings in Ulverston aforesaid lying and being at certain places there called Stainton and Stainton Gap the Cragg and Nettleslack payable yearly at the said feast amounting by the particular to eight shillings by the year and now paid and payable from the several persons following. That is to say Joan Wilson eight pence, George Wilson nine pence John Christopherson one penny, the wife of Joseph Bayliffe fourteen pence, Richard Coward one shilling four pence, James Wilson one shilling four pence, Henry Lindow eleven pence, James Lindow and William Davis ten pence, Hugh Penny, Robert Coward and Jane Geldart ten pence halfpenny And all that free rent of nine pence halfpenny going out of certain parcels of land in Osmonderley alias Osmotherley late in the tenure of Edward late Earl of Darby payable yearly at the said feast of St Martin and now payable yearly by the constable of Osmotherley aforesaid from time to time for the time being. And also all that free rent of two pence halfpenny going out of a certain parcel of land call Tilberthwaite herefofore in the tenure of Pennington payable yearly at the said feast of St Martin. And also all those free rents going out of certain parcels of land and hereditaments in Rossett heretofore in the tenure of William Hetton John Lebens, Edward Gawntound, Sir Robert Nevill knight by the particular thereof amounting to fourteen pence or thereabouts and now paid and payable by the severall persons hereafter named as following that is to say Hugh Walker one penny halfpenny, Christopher Fell two pence, Matthew Fell two pence, Alice Postlethwaite one penny, John Greaves one penny Thomas Greaves two pence, Thomas Fell two pence, William Robinson two pence and Henry Lindow one penny. And also all that free rent of fourteen pence or thereabouts be it more or less going out of certain lands in Manislarig als Mansrigg heretofore in the tenure of the said Sir Robert Nevill and now paid and payable from the persons following that is to say Myles Benson two pence, William Shakley one penny, William Ormandy two pence, John Towers one penny George Postlethwaite one penny Matthew Noble one penny William Benson three pence and William Ormandy three pence. And also all that free rent of Eighteen pence going out of some land called Addisons Land near Crake in Ulverston aforesaid and now paid and payable by the several persons following that is to say Richard Addison Nine pence James Penny seven pence Joseph Penny two pence. And also all that free rent of twelve pence going out of certain lands within the Barony of Ulverston aforesaid. All which said rents are payable at the feast of St Martin in Winter, And also all those lands, tenements and hereditaments of the tenants at will or the customary tenants of the said manor of lordship of Ulverston that is to say all that burgage croft or tenement with the appurtenances situate, lying and being in the Town of Ulverston in the said County of Lancaster now or late in the tenure or occupation of John Meramse or his assigns being of the yearly customary rent of thirteen shillings an d four pence or thereabouts And all that parcel of land or tenement with the appurtenances in Ulverston aforesaid now or late in the tenure or occupation of the said John Corker Senr or his assigns being of the yearly customary rent of four pence or thereabouts. And all that messuage, shop or tenement with the appurtenances in Ulverston aforesaid now or late in the tenure or occupation of William Kilner fellmercer apothecary or his assigns being of the yearly rent of four shillings sixpence or thereabouts and all that burgage, messuage common tements with appurtenances in Ulverston aforesaid now or late in the tenure or occupation of Margaret Woodburn widow and John Woodburn her son or one of them their or the one of their assigns being of the yearly customary rent of three shillings sixpence or thereabouts. And all that burgage, messuage or tenement with the appurtenances in Ulverston aforesaid now or late in the tenure or occupation of the said John Woodburn or Margaret Woodsburn or one of them their or the one of their assigns being of the yearly customary rent of six shillings and eight pence. And all that burgage, messuage or tenement with the appurtenances in Ulverston aforesaid now or late in the tenure or occupation of the Thomas Benson gentleman or his assigns being of the yearly customary rent of six shillings or thereabouts. And all that burgage, messuage or tenement with the appurtenances in Ulverston aforesaid now or late in the tenure or occupation of Robert Holmes weaver or his assigns being of the yearly customary rent of three shillings four pence or thereabouts. And all that burgage, messuage or tenement with the appurtenances in Ulverston aforesaid now or late in the tenure or occupation of the George Mount senior or his assigns being of the yearly customary rent of two shillings or thereabouts. And all that burgage, messuage or tenement with the appurtenances in Ulverston aforesaid now or late in the tenure or occupation of Thomas Ormandy of his assigns being of the yearly customary of three shillings eight pence of thereabouts. And all that burgage, messuage or tenement with the appurtenances in Ulverston aforesaid now or late in the tenure or occupation of Katherine Ellithorne or her assigns being of the yearly customary rent of one shilling four pence of thereabouts. And all that burgage, messuage or tenement with the appurtenances in Ulverston aforesaid now or late in the tenure or occupation of Thomas Clegg or his assigns being of the yearly customary rent of two shillings six pence or thereabouts. And all that burgage, messuage or tenement with the appurtenances in Ulverston aforesaid now or late in the tenure or occupation of Richard Atkinson carpenter of his assigns being of the yearly customary rent of four shillings or thereabouts. And all that burgage, messuage or tenement with the appurtenances in Ulverston aforesaid now or late in the tenure or occupation of George Holme glover of his assigns being of the yearly customary rent of two shillings eight pence or thereabouts. And all that burgage, messuage or tenement with the appurtenances in Ulverston aforesaid now or late in the tenure or occupation of William Clegg or his assigns being of the yearly customary rent of six shillings or thereabouts. And all that burgage, messuage or tenement with the appurtenances in Ulverston aforesaid now or late in the tenure, possession or occupation of Thomas Collinson blacksmith or his assigns being of the yearly customary rent of two shillings or thereabouts. And all that burgage, messuage or tenement with the appurtenances in Ulverston aforesaid now or late in the tenure, possession or occupation of Richard Briggs roper or his assigns being of the yearly customary rent of one shilling eight pence or thereabouts. And all that burgage, messuage or tenement with the appurtenances in Ulverston aforesaid now or late in the tenure, possession or occupation of John Ellithorne or his assigns being of the yearly customary rent of one shilling or thereabouts. And all that burgage, messuage or tenement with the appurtenances in Ulverston aforesaid now or late in the tenure, possession or occupation of Thomas Jackson or his assigns being of the yearly customary rent of five shillings or thereabouts. And all that burgage, messuage or tenement with the appurtenances in Ulverston aforesaid now or late in the tenure, possession or occupation of Margaret Jackson spinster or her assigns being of the yearly customary rent of seven pence or thereabouts. And all that burgage, messuage or tenement with the appurtenances in Ulverston aforesaid now or late in the tenure, possession or occupation of Ellin Collinson spinster or her assigns being of the yearly customary rent of threepencehalfpenny or thereabouts.

And all that burgage, messuage or tenement with the appurtenances in Ulverston aforesaid now or late in the tenure, possession or occupation of John Fell white-smith or his assigns being of the yearly customary rent of three pence halfpenny or thereabouts. And all that burgage, messuage or tenement with the appurtenances in Ulverston aforesaid now or late in the tenure, possession or occupation of William Lindow of Smithy Green or his assigns being of the yearly customary rent of Eight shillings eight pence or thereabouts. And all that barn, hempgarth or tenement with the appurtenances in Ulverston aforesaid now or late in the tenure or occupation of the said Thomas Colton or his assigns being of the yearly customary rent of six pence or thereabouts. And all that burgage, messuage or tenement with the appurtenances in Ulverston aforesaid now or late in the tenure, possession or occupation of James Stilling or his assigns being of the yearly customary rent of or thereabouts. And all that burgage close of land called Townend close or tenement with the appurtenances in Ulverston aforesaid now or late in the tenure or occupation of Roger Woodburn gentleman or his assigns being of the yearly customary rent of six shillings eight pence or thereabouts And all that burgage, of ground called Townbank Close or tenement with appurtenances in Ulverston aforesaid now or late in the occupation of William Wilson carpenter and his assigns being of the yearly customary rent of six shillings and eight pence or thereabouts. And all that parcel of ground or tenement with appurtenances in Ulverston aforesaid now or late in occupation of George Millerson or his assigns being of the yearly customary rent of two shillings or thereabouts. And all that burgage or tenement with appurtenances now or late in the occupation of Richard Fell mercer or his assigns being of the yearly customary rent of four shillings or thereabouts. And all that tenement or parcel of land called Abraham Dale with appurtenances now or late in the occupation of Henry Leetham or his assigns being of the yearly customary rent of two shillings and eight pence or thereabouts and all and singular the rents fines upon death alienaroid change and alteration of lord or tenant boons, gressons town terms the one boon shearing in harvest and the other work of the tenants, dues, duties labours, services whatsoever of the said customary tenants of the said manor or lordship of Ulverston and every one of them their and every of their heirs and assigns. And all that Tarnside yearly sold in the moss called Plumpton Moss lately in tenure of John Corker of yearly rent or value of eight shillings. And also all that piece of land called Anne's Myre in the tenure of the relict of John Dobson on yearly rent or value of three pence. And also all that Terricide yearly sold in the said moss called Plumpton Moss and Ulver-ston Moss late in tenure of William Bardsey and now in tenure of Christopher Anderton of Bardsea Hall in the said County of Lancaster Esquire and William Salthouse or their assigns lying near a certain place in the same moss called Rayme Hill of yearly rent or value of two shillings which is now paid and payable by them yearly as follows videliset the said Christopher Anderton one shilling and nine pence and the said William Salthouse three pence. And also all that moiety or half part of one message or tenement in Plumpton together with all singular the appurtenances of the same belonging. And also the moiety of one messuage or tenement called Plumptonhead with four acres of land in tenure of Matthew Noble together with sheep pasture in the wood there. And also the moiety of another messuage in Plumpton with appurtenances with one acre of land severally enclosed lots in tenure Christopher Ellithorne or his assigns. And also the moiety of another messuage or tenement with eight acres and a half of meadow with appurtenances near Trydley in Plumpton aforesaid late in the tenure of Rowland Cowhird or his assigns together by the particulars thereof menconed to be of the yearly rent or value of thirtyone shillings and eight pence. And also all those two acres and a half of arable enclosed land late in the tenure of the said Sir Robert Neville or his assigns. And also those six acres and a half of land late in the occupation of Robert Wyre or his assigns. and also those seven acres of land lying in the North part of Galabry als Gallobarrow parcel of the said Manor of Ulverston together by the particulars thereof of yearly rent of ten shillings. And also those saltpits and salt-coats being within the barony of Ulverston aforesaid of the yearly rent of seven shillings or thereabouts by the particulars thereof. And also all the parcel of landof an acre or thereabouts lying near Flan heretofor in the tenure of John Billings gentleman called Kilnehall in Blawith within the barony and manor of Ulverston containing by estimation one acre and a half of arable land and pasture now or late in the tenure of Thomas Brockbank of Tottlebank in Blawith aforesaid of the yearly rent of six pence. And all that cottage situate in Ulverston aforesaid calle Ellers heretofor in the tenure of John Holme and now in the tenure of Alice wife of the said Thomas Clegg and her assigns of the yearly rent of two pence. And also all that moiety or one half of all and singular of the messuage, shop, barns, kilns, lands and other heredidataments microuched within Ulverston aforesaid the whole being by the particulars thereof menconed to be of the yearly rent of three shillings or thereabouts. And servant right and being within the town of Ulverston aforesaid in the several tenures of the persons following that is to say one messuage and barn with appurtenances now in the tenure or occupation of Alice Ellithorne widow or her assigns of the yearly rent of six pence. One shop with appurtenances now or late in the occupation of John Fell of Daltongate or his assigns of the yearly rent of of nine pence or thereabouts. One other shop there with appurtenances now or late in the occupation of the said William Kilner apothecary or his assigns of the yearly rent of four pence or thereabouts. One kiln situated in the Ellers with appurtenances now or late in the occupation of Thomas Marr of Rattenrow or his assigns of the yearly rent of eight pence or thereabouts. One barn with appurtenances now or late in the occupation of William Wilson and his assigns of the yearly rent of four pence or thereabouts. One parcel of land with appurtenances now or late in the occupation of William Clegg or his assigns of the yearly rent of two pence or thereabouts.. One barn and garth with appurtenances now or late in the occupation of John Benson of Bottoms or his assigns of the yearly rent of eight pence or thereabouts. Moiety or half part all the moss and turbary in the said Plumpton Moss or Ulverston Moss valie eight pounds or thereabout yearly rent to be forty shillings or thereabouts. And also all those free burgage houses shoppes buildings and hereditaments with the appurtenances situate and lying in the said town of Ulverston now or late in the possession of diverse persons hereinafter named who held or do hold the same by leased or leases for year or years from the said Charles Fell and Hannah Fell or one of them their or one of their assigns. That is to say all that the burgage house wherewith the said Hannah Fell did lately dwell and inhabit in Ulverston aforesaid with one shop adjoining late in possession of John Richardson and now in possession of Thomas Boulton, and one other shop also adjoining now or late in possession of Lawrence Kilner brasier all which houses and shops aforesaid are abutting on William Fell's shop and the marketplace on the South side, the said William Kilner's new house on the East side and the Little Beck running through the town of Ulverston on the North side and the king's highway thereon the West part. And also all that and those the burgage house messuage tenements now commonly called and known by the name or names of the Stonehouse and barn, kiln, wifehouse and two gardens, the hempgarth with appurtenances lying and being between the becks in the said town of Ulverston purchased by the said Thomas Fell esquire of William Corker and adjoining the highway on the West and to the Great Beck or river running down the said town of Ulverston with the East End and to Thomas Fisher baker's house and garth as to the South and William Fisher's house and hempgarth upon the North which same house, shop and premises were all lately in the several possessions of John Richardson, William Fell, Lawrence Kilner, James Geldart and Samuel Sandys some or one of them their or some of their lessee or lessees. And also two shops late in possession of John Fell mercer and Alice Cowper now in possession of William Fisher mercer and the said Alice Cowper the premises lessee leases butting upon the said Richard Fell's shop upon the west end upon said John Fell's on the Northeast and the marketplace in Ulverston aforesaid upon the south and the king's highway on the east. And also all and singular the lands, tenements and hereditaments of the customary tenants of the said manor and lordship of Blawith that is to say the messuage and tenement with appurtenances situate, lying and being at Oxenclose in Blawith situated in parish of Ulverston in the said County of Lancaster now or late in tenure and occupation of John Wilson or his assigns at the yearly customary rent of six shillings and one penny. And all that messuage or tenement with appurtenances (Here starts the third membrane) in Blawith aforesaid now or late in the tenure and occupation of Leonard Taylor or his assigns being of the yearly rent of six shillings seven pence halfpenny. And all that messuage or tenement with appurtenances in Blawith aforesaid now or late in the tenure and occupation of William Redhead or his assigns being of the yearly rent of two shillings eight pence halfpenny And all that cottage and parcel of moss ground with appurtenances in Blawith aforesaid now or late in the tenure and occupation of Matthew Redhead or his assigns being of the yearly rent of a half penny farthing. And all that parcel and tenement with appurtenances in Blawith aforesaid now or late in the tenure and occupation of Thomas Brockbank or his assigns being of the yearly rent of nine pence halfpenny. And all that messuage or tenement with appurtenances at Stable Harvey in Blawith aforesaid now or late in the tenure and occupation of the said Thomas Brockbank or his assigns being of the yearly rent of four shillings and nine pence And all that messuage or tenement with appurtenances at Stable Harvey in Blawith aforesaid now or late in the tenure and occupation of John Chamley or his assigns being of the yearly rent of four shillings and two pence or thereabouts And all that messuage or tenement with appurtenances at Stable Harvey in Blawith aforesaid now or late in the tenure and occupation of Richard Park or his assigns being of the yearly rent of one shilling and a farthing. And all that messuage or tenement with appurtenances at Stable Harvey in Blawith aforesaid now or late in the tenure and occupation of Thomas Park or his assigns being of the yearly rent of thirteen pence halfpenny farthing. And all that messuage or tenement with appurtenances at Stable Harvey in Blawith aforesaid now or late in the tenure and occupation of Richard Fisher or his assigns being of the yearly rent of three shillings and one running penny yearly as customary to each of the said tenants. And all that messuage or tenement with appurtenances in Blawith aforesaid now or late in the tenure and occupation of James Penny or his assigns being of the yearly rent of five shillings and four pence. And all that messuage or tenement with appurtenances in Blawith aforesaid now or late in the tenure and occupation of Robert Redhead or his assigns being of the yearly rent of twelve pence. And all that messuage or tenement with appurtenances in Blawith aforesaid now or late in the tenure and occupation of Nicholas Penny or his assigns being of the yearly rent of seven shillings and eight pence farthing. And all that parcel of lands or tenement with appurtenances in Blawith aforesaid now or late in the tenure and occupation of John Fisher or his assigns being of the yearly rent of two shillings and seven pence. And all that messuage croft or tenement with appurtenances in Blawith aforesaid now or late in the tenure and occupation of John Sawrey or his assigns being of the yearly rent of four pence half penny. And all that two parcels of land or tenement with appurtenances in Blawith aforesaid now or late in the tenure and occupation of Henry Sawrey or his assigns being of the yearly rent of twelve pence half pence. And all that messuage or tenement with appurtenances in Blawith aforesaid now or late in the tenure and occupation of Margaret Redhead widow or her assigns being of the yearly rent of one shilling and six pence. And all that parcel of land or tenement with appurtenances in Blawith aforesaid now or late in the tenure and occupation of James Wilson or his assigns being of the yearly rent of four pence. And all that parcel of land or tenement with appurtenances in Blawith aforesaid now or late in the tenure and occupation of Richard Dodgson or his assigns being of the yearly rent of eleven pence. And all that messuage or tenement with appurtenances in Blawith aforesaid now or late in the tenure and occupation of William Addison or his assigns being of the yearly rent of four shillings and two pence. And all that parcel of land or tenement with appurtenances in Blawith aforesaid now or late in the tenure and occupation of Robert Towers or his assigns being of the yearly rent of four shillings and one penny. And all that messuage or tenement with appurtenances in Blawith aforesaid now or late in the tenure and occupation of William Poole or his assigns being of the yearly rent of eight pence. And all that messuage garth or tenement with appurtenances in Blawith aforesaid now or late in the tenure and occupation of Robert Redhead blacksmith or his assigns being of the yearly rent of six pence. And all that parcel of meadow land with appurtenances in Blawith aforesaid now or late in the tenure and occupation of Thomas Fisher or his assigns being of the yearly rent of two pence. And all that close parcel of ground with appurtenances in Blawith aforesaid called Gibbsstogize being of the yearly rent of six pence half-penny. And all that messuage or tenement with appurtenances in Blawith aforesaid now or late in the tenure and occupation of Mary Sherwen widow or her assigns being of the yearly rent of two pence. And all that messuage or tenement with appurtenances in Blawith aforesaid now or late in the tenure and occupation of Richard Penny or his assigns being of the yearly rent of two pence half penny. And all that messuage or tenement with appurtenances in Blawith aforesaid now or late in the tenure and occupation of William Kirby or his assigns being of the yearly rent of one penny. And all that parcels of ground or tenement with appurtenances in Blawith aforesaid now or late in the tenure and occupation of James Stephenson or his assigns being of the yearly rent of four pence. And all that messuage or tenement with appurtenances in Blawith aforesaid now or late in the tenure and occupation of William Turner his assigns being of the yearly rent of two pence. And all that parcels of land and pasturage or tenement with appurtenances in Blawith aforesaid now or late in the tenure and occupation of Thomas Russell or his assigns being of the yearly rent of eight pence. And all that mossy ground or tenement with appurtenances in Blawith aforesaid now or late in the tenure and occupation of John Wilson cooper or his assigns being of the yearly rent of one penny. And all those parcels of land or tenement with appurtenances in Blawith aforesaid now or late in the tenure and occupation of John Loggan or his assigns being of the yearly rent of ten pence farthing. And all that meadow ground with appurtenances in Blawith aforesaid now or late in the tenure and occupation of William Swainson or his assigns being of the yearly rent of one shilling. And all that messuage or tenement with appurtenances in Blawith aforesaid now or late in the tenure and occupation of Thomas Brockbank or his assigns being of the yearly rent of six pence one penny halfpenny farthing. And all that cottage or tenement with appurtenances in Blawith aforesaid now or late in the tenure and occupation of Jennett Stewart widow or his assigns being of the yearly rent of two pence. And all that messuage or tenement with appurtenances in Blawith aforesaid now or late in the tenure and occupation of William Penny or his assigns being of the yearly rent of nineteen pence half penny. And all that parcel of ground with appurtenances in Blawith aforesaid now or late in the tenure and occupation of Robert Gibson or his assigns being of the yearly rent of one half penny. And all that parcel of arable and meadow land or tenement with appurtenances in Blawith aforesaid now or late in the tenure and occupation of John Turner or his assigns being of the yearly rent of one penny. And all that messuage or tenement with appurtenances in Nibthwaite in Furness Fells in the County of Lancaster now or late in the tenure and occupation of William Fleming or his assigns being of the yearly rent of five shillings and three shillings seven pence halfpenny. And all that messuage or tenement with appurtenances in Helpark and Bethecar in Furness Fells now or late in the tenure and occupation of Joseph Dodgeson or his assigns being of together with the yearly rent of two pence for Greenhow and perquisates of court at Helpark aforesaid with yearly rent of fourteen shillings and seven pence halfpenny And all that parcel of ground or tenement with appurtenances in Bethecar aforesaid now or late in the tenure and occupation of James Towers or his assigns being of the yearly rent of thirteen pence half penny farthing. And all that parcel of ground or tenement with appurtenances in Bethecar aforesaid now or late in the tenure and occupation of John Chamney or his assigns being of the yearly rent of two shillings three pence half penny. (here begins membrane 4)

And all that messuage and tenement with the appurtenances lying or being at Ashlack in Furnessfells aforesaid now or late in the tenure or occupation of Richard Corker or his assigns being of the yearly rent of three shillings eight pence half-penny farthing or thereabouts. And all that messuage and tenement with appurtenances situate lying at Ashlack in Furnessfells aforesaid now or late in the tenure or occupation of John Corker and his assigns being of the yearly rent of three shillings eight pence halfpenny farthing or thereabouts. And all that parcel of ground with appurtenances lying or being at Nibthwaite in Furnessfells aforesaid now or late in the tenure or occupation of William Dodgson or his assigns being the yearly rent of one shilling and threepence or thereabouts and all that and those parcels of land or tenement with appurtenances lying and being at Helpark in Furnessfells aforesaid now or late in the tenure or occupation of Garnett Pennington being of the yearly rent of eleven pence or thereabouts. And all that parcels of land or tenement lying and being at Helpark in Furnessfells aforesaid now or late in the tenure or occupation of William Dobson or his assigns being of the yearly rent of two pence or thereabouts And all that messuage garth and tenement with appurtenances lying and being at Helpark in Furness Fells now or late in the tenure or occupation of Hugh Dobson or his assigns being of the yearly rent of one penny or thereabouts. And all and singular the rent fines upon death alienaroid change and alteroid of lord and tenant running twice or gressons running penny Greenhues Mills silver renthenns boones and all other dues duties labours and service whatsoever of the said customary tenants within Furnessfells and the mannor of Blawith aforesaid and of them their and every of their heirs and assignes And all that the free fishing and several fishing with appurtenances in and upon Thirstonwater or Coniston water within the several parish of Ulverston Dalton Hawkshead & Coniston in the said County of Lancaster or any of them at Otterstock Nappen Tree and Watergarth or in any other place in or upon the said water and the banke and grounds thereunto belonging And also all that the free fishing and in the River Leven and in and upon the sands called Leven Sands in the said County of Lancaster with the appurtenances Together with all and all manner of instruments and materials for fishing whatsoever to the said free fishings and several fishings or any of them or any part thereof belonging or in anywise appertaining And all that and those the grounds called Oxenhouse Greatwood with the appurtenances lying and being at Oxenhouse in Blawith aforesaid in the said County of Lancaster between the cornfields lying on the South side of the said Oxenhouses Greatwood and the fellend with all the woods underwoods and trees and the ground and soil thereof and all other the rights members and appurtenance thereunto belonging or in anywise appertaining. Which said Oxenhouse Greatwood was heretofore in the several tenures possession or occupations of Edward Jackson, William Willson and Robert Redhead as customary tenants thereof and there title thereto was purchased by the said Thomas Fell then lord thereof as by three several deeds thereof from them severally to him made may appear And also all that close of pasture and woody ground and appurtences called the Glasse Knott with all the woods underwoods and trees and the ground and soil thereof And the third part of half acre of meadow (be it more or less) lying or being near the Abbot Oakes Green commonly called the Champney Meadow with the appurtenances both lying within Furnessfells in the said County of Lancaster and being heretofore purchased by the said Thomas Fell then lord thereof from Richard Burnes and before the said purchase thereof being parcels of one customary tenement at Ashlack in Furnessfells aforesaid And a third part of all the common of pasture belonging to the aforesaid tenement called Ashlack with the appurtenances And also all those three watercornmills with their and every of their appurtenances situate and being in Ulverston aforesaid in the said Country of Lancaster commonly called or known by the severall name or names following the Corn Mill als the Town Mill, the Overmill als the Ure Mill and the Little Mill als Bottom Mill And all that the moiety or one half the watercornmill and kill with all their rights members and appurtenances commonly called and known by name or names of Newland Mill and Kilne and the peathouse and other buildings situate standing and being within the parish of Ulverston aforesaid upon the common near the highway which leadeth directly from Ulverston Town to Arrad Foot. Together with all and singular messuages mansion houses edifices structures barns gardens orchards common ways paths weare milldams millhouse and floodgates of the water water courses rivulets streams pools farnes banks fishings fishing places liberties of fishing waste woods underwoods and trees with all the suit to mills sockengrist moulture toll customs millstones millwheels chestsarks hoppers baskets farms, perks measures millparks gawlocks spades hammers leasewood and timber ladders and all other instruments utensils and materials whatsoever for and in the said mills rents reversions rights furrisdintions franchises liberties priviledges profits commodities and emoluments whatsoever with all and singular rights members and appurtenances of what said nature and sorts over or by what name or names or addition of names they may be called reputed taken or known situate lying and being renewing happening or remaining within the villages parishes places or hamlets aforesaid or within any of them or elsewhere to the said three water corn mills and the said moiety of the said other water corn mill and kiln and other buildings thereto adjacent called Newland Mill and Kiln within the said parish of Ulverston and the rest of the same mills and premises next above by these presents granted or mentioned or intended to be granted or to any of them or to any part or parcel thereof as respectively belonging appertaining indent or appendant or as member part or parcel thereof or any of the respectively heretofore had known accepted occupied used demised enjoyed or reputed And the reveroid and reverous remainder and remainders whatsoever of the same premises and every or any part and parcel thereof depending or expecting upon any demise or grant demises and grants thereof and of every or any part or parcel thereof for the term or terms of life or lives years or years or otherwise being of record or not of record And also all the rents and yearly profits whatsoever reserved out and payable upon any demise or grants of the same premises or any part or parcel thereof And also all and singular the moss mossground and turbary with the appurtenances of them the said Charles Fell Mary his wife Margaret Fox Hannah Fell John Rous Margaret his wife Abraham Morrice Isabella his wife, William Mead Sarah his wife Thomas Lower Mary his wife, Susanna Fell Daniel Abraham Rachael his wife James Greaves Isabella his wife

Thomas Colton and Mary his wife and every of them lying and being in Ulverston Moss Plumpton Moss and elsewhere in the said County of Lancaster now in the possession and occupation of the said Charles Fell Hannah Fell and Daniel Abraham or any of them their or their assigns or to the said messuages lands tenements mills and premises hereby granted or intended to be granted or to any part or parcel thereof belonging or appertaining or therewithal and with any part or parcel thereof now or heretofore usually occupied or demised or accepted reputed taken or known to be as part parcel or member thereof of belonging thereunto. And also all and singular the tithes of corn grain and sheaves hemp hay flax wool and same and all other tithable matters whatsoever tyth mouleture easter dues easter reckonings oblation obventions portions and penions marw or compositions for tythe and all tythes as well great and smallor minute tythes personal pradial or mixt and all and all manner of other tythes whatsoever yearly and from time to time arising growing renewing increasing raising or happening in upon or out of all and singular the mannors messuages lands tenements mills hereditaments and premises with the appurtenances herein granted or mentioned or intended hereby or by the said intended fine and recovery to be granted or in or on or out of every or any part or parcel thereof with their and every of their appurtenances. And all or singular the manors or lordships or reputed manors or lordships messuages burgages houses edifices buildings cottages lands tenements meadows pastures feedings water corn mills windmills ironmills furnaces forges ironworks fishings fishing places woods woody grounds mosses moores marshes commons common of pasture and turbary rents fines boones dues duties devised royalties liberties priviledges advantages emoluments and other hereditaments of them the said Charles Fell and Mary his wife Margaret Fox Hannah Fell John Rous Margaret his wife Abraham Morrice Isabella his wife, William Mead Sarah his wife Thomas Lower Mary his wife, William Ingram and Susanna his wife James Greaves and Isasbella his wife Thomas Colton and Mary his wife and every of them with their rights members and appurtenances situate and lying and being in the parishes townships villages and places of Ulverston Swarthmoor Dragley Beck Hawkswell Blawith Lowick Pennington Urswick Dalton Coulton Hawkshead Nibthwaite Bethacre Furness and Furnesfells in the said County of Lancaster or elsewhere

(beginning of membrane 5)

The same county whereof or wherein the said Charles Fell, Mary his wife Margaret Fox, Hannah Fell, John Rous Margaret his wife, Abraham Morrice Isabella his wife, William Mead Sarah his wife, Thomas Lower Mary his wife, Susannah Fell, Jam,es Geaves, Isabella his wife, Thomas Colton and Mary his wife or any of them or any other person or persons to their or any of their use or uses or in trust for them or any of them or are seized of any estate or inheritance and which was the inheritance of the said Thomas Fell the grandfather and George Fell father of the said Charles Fell or either of them together with all and singular the messuages houses burgages barns stables outhouses, dovecoates, edifices structured buildings cotts crofts curtilages, cottages orchards, gardens garths hemplands hortyards lands tenements tarns pools meadows pastures feeding learures demesne lands commons common of pasture and turbary, moores mosses marishes waste hearths furrowaies paths easements woods underwoods timber woods grounds and trees on the ground and soyle of the same, profits commodities banks rivers waters watercourses and the leading of water fish fishinge liberty of fishing fishing places all instruments of fishing whatsoever, fowling, nutering, suite sockengrist moulture millhouse floodgates streams free water courses mines quarries delfs rents revenues and services rent charges rent serke the rents and services as well of the free as the customary tenants the due boone shearing in harvest and other work of the tenants and other inhabitants the said mannors and either of them, the fines there upon the death alienaroid/and change of Lord and tenant and all other fines whatsoever, the rents and services reserved upon demise or grant of the premises or any part thereof, the rent of the fee farms the mosse rents customes annuityes tiheated releise herriotts amerciaments the certaine rents and common fines of the court leet or view of frankpledge the profits and perquisites of the courts and leetes and all that belong or which hereafter may or ought to belong to the court lets and view frankpledges all the goods and chattels that are waived or strayed within the said mannors or either of them in the goods and chattels of felons as well as of themselves as of the felons that are fugitive persons outlawed attainted condemned and put to the exigent deodands estovers common of estovers fairs markets tolls customes rights to royalties ononollart jurisdictions franchises liberties privilledges advantages emoluments rents rent renthouses townterms running pennys greenhires dues boones services duties reversions and chattels how heriditaments within the said mannors lordships villages fields parishes places or hamlets aforesaid or within any of them or elsewhere to the premises or any part or owen parcel whereof any way belonging or appertaining or commonly interpreted reputed to belong or appertaining to the said mannors messuages mills fishings lands tenements hereditaments and premises or any part or parcel thereof respectively or now or at any time heretofore had knoone accepted occupied demised used or reputed as member part or parcel of the off premised. And the reversion and reversions whatsoever of all and singular the premises and of every part thereof expectant or depending of in or upon any demise of grant demises or grants heretofor made thereof or any part or parcel thereof for term or terms of life lives or years or otherwise and the rents and yearly profits whatsoever reserved due or payable upon all every or any such demises or grants of the premises or any part or parcel thereof. And all the Seignory lordsright and other estate right tithe interest claming and demand whatsoever of them the said Charles Fell Mary his wife Margaret Fox Hannah Fell John Rous Margaret his wife Abraham Morrice Isabella his wife, William Mead Sarah his wife, Thomas Lower Mary his wife Susannah Fell, James Greaves Isabella his wife, Thomas Colton and Mary his wife and of all every or any of them in land or equity or otherwise howsoever of ni and unto the said premises and every or any part and parcel thereof together with all such deeds charters, evidences, transcripts of fines and recovered court rolls court books scripts, muniments and writings whatsoever as forth mentioned or concere the same premises with the appurtenances and every or any part thereof which they or any of them have or hath in their or any of their custody or rann? Come by without suits in law. **Excepting** All those three other watercorn mils and one corn windmill with the appurtenances late in the possession or occupation of the said Charles Fell and Hannah Fell or any of them their or the one of their assignes and now in the possession of the said Thomas Lower or his assigns commonly called and known by the names of the Littlemill Roosemill, Orgrave mill and the windmill all lying or being in the parish of Dalton aforesaid **To have and to hold** all and singular the said mannors lordships messuages lands tenements rents reversions mills fishings hereditaments and premises here in before mentioned and intended to be hereby granted bargained, sold aliened enfeoffed remised released ratified and confirmed with their and every of their appurtenances except as before expressed unto them the said Richard Rawlinson and Thomas Richardson of Whinfield and their heirs to the use of them the said Richard Rawlinson and Thomas Richardson of Whinfield and their heirs To the intent and purpose that they the said Richard Rawlinson and Thomas Richardson of Whinfield may hereby and by the fines hereby agreed to belovyed become person tenants of the freehold of all and singular the above mentioned hereditaments and premises And the said Richard Rawlinson and Thomas Richardson of Whinfield or the survivor of them at the next assize or great general sessions of pleas holden for the County Pallatine of Lancaster before their Matyes Justices there shall and do permit and suffer the said Thomas Richardson of Rownehead and John Corker to bring and sue out of the King and Queens Matyes Court of Chancery within the said County Pallatine of Lancaster according to the course of common recordies for the assurance of Lands within the said County Palatine one or more writt or writs of entry in the post against the said Richard Rawlinson and Thomas Richardson of Whinfield returnable before theire said Matyes Justices there whereby the said Thomas Richardson of Rownehead and John Corker shall and may demand against the said Richard Rawlinson and Thomas Richardson of Whinfield all the said mannors lordships messuages lands tenements rents reversions mills fishings heridatments and all and singular other premises by such proper names as shall be advised and that the said Richard Rawlinson and Thomas Richardson of Whinfield to the said writ or writs shall appear before the said justices at the day of the return thereof in proper person or by attorny lawfully authorised in that belf after which said appearance the said Thomas Richardson of Rownehead and John Corker upon the said writt or writs shall declare against the said Richard Rawlinson and Thomas Richardson of Whinfield after which declaration the said Richard Rawlinson and Thomas Richardson of Whinfield shall have defence and shall vouch the said Charles Fell who shall likewise appear gratis and after defence shall vouch over to warranty the common vouchee who shall likewise appear and enter into the warranty and after imparlance shall make default and depart in contempt of the court so that a good and perfect recovery and judgement shall and may berrecoupon has against the said Richard Rawlinson and Thomas Richardson of Whinfield and so over against the common vouchee according to the course of common recoveryes in like cases used and judgement and execution shall be thereupon had by the said Thomas Richardson of Rownehead and John Corker And it is hereby declared and agreed and between all the said parties of these presents that from and after the perfecting of the said recovery or recoveries the said recovery or recoveries so or in any other manner to be had or suffered and every other recoverys fines conveyances and assurances in the law heretofor had made leveyed suffered or executed by and between the parties to these presents any of them or ioner unto they or any of them shall be parties or pelvyes of the said mannors lordships messuages lands tenements rents reversions mills fishings hereditaments and premises or any of them shall be ownere and are hereby declared and so are and were incontend intended to be and ennre ane the said the said recoverys named or to be named and their heirs shall from thenceforth stand and be seized of the said mannors lands tenements rents reversions mills fishings hereditaments and premises and every of them to the uses intents and purposes upon the trust and with and under the provisos limitsanoids and agreement hereinafter mentioned and declared concerning the same and to and no other use intent or purpose whatsoever that is to say as (Here begins membrane 6)

As for and concerning sum parcels of the said premises as by two several indentures made or mentioned to be made the fifth and sixth days of March which was the eighteenth year of the late majesty King Charles the second between the said George Fell sercuses of the one part and Margaret Fox matrix of the said George Fell deceased of the other part were limited and assigned granted and conveyed to the said Margaret Fox in lieu and satisfaction of the dower of the said Margaret or otherwise for the better or more perfect assuring such annual or yearly payment as were mentioned and expressed to be granted and payable to the said Margaret and her assigns To the use of the said Margaret Fox for such interest term of years and estate as therein and thereby respectively limited granted and appointed And as for and concerning all the rest and residue of the said mannors lordships messuages lands tenements rents reversions mills fishings hereditaments and premises no interest or estate is limited by the said recited deeds to the said Margaret Fox. Except as before excepted its also and concerning all and singular the said premises together with the easements and commodities thereto belonging so to be limited after the expiration and determination of such her said interest and estate which is not intended hereby to be in any way prejudiced or unimpaired To the use and behoofe of the said Daniel Abraham his heirs and assigns for ever And the said Charles Fell for himself his heirs executors and assigns and every of them dost covenant promise and grant to and with the said Daniel Abraham his heirs and assigns by these presents in manner and form following that is to say that he the said Charles Fell for himself together with the said Mary his wife, Margaret Fox Hannah Fell James Greaves Isabella his wife John Rouse Margaret his wife Abraham Morrice Isabella his wife, William Mead Sarah his wife, Thomas Lower Mary his wife, William Ingram Susanna his wife and Thomas Colton and Mary his wife now is and standeth lawfully and rightfully seized of and in all and singular the said mannors lordships messuages lands tenements rents reversions mills fishings hereditaments and premises of a good sure absolute of indefeasible estate of inheritance and has himself or heretogether with his the said Mary his wife, Margaret Fox Hannah Fell James Greaves Isabella his wife John Rouse Margaret his wife Abraham Morrice Isabella his wife, William Mead Sarah his wife, Thomas Lower Mary his wife, William Ingram Susanna his wife and Thomas Colton and Mary his wife have full power and lawful and absolute authority to grant convey and assign all and every the said mannors lordships messuages lands tenements rents reversions mills fishings hereditaments and premises to the several and respective uses intents and purposes other than before limited and declared And that all and every the aforesaid mannors lordships messuages lands tenements rents reversions mills fishings hereditaments and premises with there and every of there rights members and appurtenances except as before excepted shall and may from time to time and at all times for ever hereafter remain continue and be to the several and respective uses and purposes herein before declared and contained free and clear and freely and clearly acquired saved the Harmclose and discharged of and from all former gifts grants bargains sales leases mortgages jointures uses dowers intailed debts recognisences judgments expenses escrourous and of and from all former estates titled charges and incumbrances whatsoever had made committed done or suffered before the said Charles Fell or the said George Fell his father or the said Thomas Fell his grandfather or either of them or any other person or persons lawfully claiming or to claim from by him them or either of them or any of the said parties to this present indenture And the said Hannah Fell James Greaves Isabella his wife John Rouse Margaret his wife Abraham Morrice Isabella his wife, William Mead Sarah his wife, Thomas Lower Mary his wife, William Ingram Susanna his wife and Thomas Colton and Mary his wife for themselves and their respective wives severally and not jointly and for their several and respective heirs executors and administrators and no one for the act and deed or for the heirs executors and administrators of the other overpurnant promise and grant to and with the said Daniel Abraham his heirs and assigns and to and with every of them by these presents that neither she the said Hannah Fell nor the said James Greaves Isabella his wife John Rouse Margaret his wife Abraham Morrice Isabella his wife, William Mead Sarah his wife, Thomas Lower Mary his wife, William Ingram Susanna his wife nor the said Thomas Colton and Mary his wife have or either of them hath at any time heretofore made done or committed any or matter of thing whereby or by means where of the said mannors lordships messuages lands tenements rents reversions mills fishings hereditaments and premises mentioned to be hereby before granted and released or any parcel or parcels there of are in or shall or may be empeached charged engaged or incumbered in the charge estate or otherwise And the said Charles Fell and his heirs and also for every of the said parties and their heirs and the said parties for themselves and their wives and respective heirs do covenant and agree in manner as aforesaid that they shall and will from time to time and at all times hereafter during the space of seven years to be accounted from the date hereof at the request cost and charges in the law of the said Daniel Abraham or his heirs do make and execute or cause or promise to be made done or eyecure all and every such further and other out and onto conveyances and assurances in the law for the further and better conveying and assuring the said mannors lordships messuages lands tenements rents reversions mills fishings hereditaments and premises to the severall and respective uses intents and purposes here before declared and set forth as by the council learned in law of the said Daniel Abraham his heirs or assigns reasonably devised advised or required Provided that such further assurances contain no other of further covenants or warranties than in these presents are mentioned and expressed And the said Hannah Fell for herself and her heirs doth further covenant and agree in manner as aforesaid that she shall and will from time to time and at all times save harmless and indemnify the said Daniel Abraham his heirs and assigns and the said mills messuages and all and singular the said premises hereby granted and confirmed of and from one judgement had and obtained within Majesty's court of Kings Bench and the term of which was in the year of the reign of his late majesty King Charles the second by Edward Cooke deceased citizen and woollen draper of London for the sum of six thousand pounds besides damages and cost of suite against the said George Fell deceased late husband of the said Hannah Fell and against Elizabeth Tomlinson sole executive of the said Edward Cooke deceased from whom and whose executors the said Hannah Fell shall and will at any time or time hereafter at the expense of the said Daniel Abraham his heirs and assigns procure such release and discharge of the said judgement or satisfaction or otherwise thereupon to be entered or otherwise the same to be assigned every to such person or persons in such manner the council learned in law of the said Daniel Abraham his heirs and assigns shall reasonably advise In witness whereof the parties first above named to their present indenture.

Signatures Ja Greaves Abr Morrice Isabella Morrice Willm Mead Mary Mead William Ingram.

APPENDIX F
PART OF THOMAS PETTY'S SORTING OUT OF THE AFFAIRS OF THOMAS ABRAHAM 1759

Seven part indenture 9th February 1759. This Document is at Friends House

This indenture of seven parts:

1. John Lewthwaite and Peter Gale merchants of Whitehaven Cumberland assignees the estates and effects of Thomas Abraham late Whitehaven aforesaid a bankrupt
2. Thomas Abraham and Ellen his wife
3. Alexander Hoskins of Papcastle gentleman
4. Henry Bainbridge of Knaresbrough gentleman
5. Anthony Ponsonby merchant Whitehaven
6. Peter Nicholson late Dublin merchant now of Whitehaven
7. Thomas Petty gentleman Ulverston

Whereas by indenture of lease and release 23rd 24th December 1743 the release being:

tripartite :-

1/ Nicholas Dodgson of Hawthorn County Durham gentleman & Warren Maude then before of Sunderland by the Sea and late of Sunny-side in Bishop Wearmouth coal fitter

2/ John Abraham gentleman Swarthmoor Hall Ulverston County Lancaster

3/ Sir William Wentworth Bt Bretton Hall in County Yorkshire

Swarthmoor Hall and other premises sold to Sir William Wentworth his heirs and assignes for ever with the proviso and condition to make void the same. John Abraham who was then entitled to the equity of redemption could void the indenture if he paid Sir William Wentworth £6000 plus interest

And whereas by indenture of lease and release 23rd 24th December 1743 re payment of £6000 between 1/ John Abraham gentleman Swarthmoor Hall & 2/ Sir William Wentworth

And whereas other indenture of lease and release 26th 27th December 1743

1/ John Abraham of Swarthmoor Halll

2/ James Collins of Knaresbrough gentleman

Sale of messuages, cottages in Ulverston, Manchester and parish of Manchester and elsewhere in Lancashire redeemable on payment of £640 by John Abraham

And Whereas by indenture 11th 12 February 1746

1/ John Abraham gentleman Swarthmoor Hall Ulverston, County of Lancaster

2/ Thomas Abraham grocer Whitehaven

Whereas John Abraham was seized of the capital messuage or manor house called Swarthmoor Halland the demesne or demain in Ulverston aforesaid and various other tenements lands mills and hereditaments whereof there was now a mortgage of £6000 and also a charge of £600 as provision for the seven younger children of John Abraham and Sarah his wife settled upon their marriage to be paid to such younger children after the death of the said John Abraham.

John Abraham and Sarah his wife to advance Thomas in the world granted him Swarthmoor Hall, Thomas Abraham undertaking the debts of the said John Abraham in a schedule inserted (but never inserted) and also Thomas Abraham said John Abraham and Sarah his wife for their joint lives and the survivor of them interest on the £600 charged for the said younger children at £5 in the hundred clear of all taxes and deductions half yearly on 11th November and 28th March with the first payment 11th of November next. John Abraham and Sarah his wife transfer to said Thomas Abraham their capital messuage of mansion house called Swarthmoor Hall containing 250 acres land more or less and also those three water corn mills Over Mill, Town Mill and Ellers Mill situate in the parish of Ulverston aforesaid to Thomas Abraham

And whereas Indenture of lease and release 8th 9th May 1752

1/ Thomas Abraham grocer of Whitehaven

2/ Peter Nicholson merchant City of Dublin

Thomas Abraham for £1700 granted by said Peter Nicholson assigns all that premises in the said last above in part related indenture of lease and release mentioned to be granted and released (the shop in Ulverston excepted) redeemable on payment of £1700 and interest

The said Peter Nicholson by certain other indentures of lease and release 12th 13th June 1752 mentioned to be made between said Peter Nicholson merchant City of Durham and Matthias Gale and John Bell merchants both City of London.

Said premises redeemable nevertheless by 13th December next by payment of £1700 plus interest

Whereas by certain Memoranda of Agreement subscribed the last at in said Indenture by said Thomas Abraham and Peter Nicholson and stated whereas the said Thomas Abraham stood indebted to the the said Peter Nicholson for £288 over and above the sum of £1700

Thomas Abraham agreed to add the £288 to the sum recorded in the Indenture and whereas the several sums of money due were not or any part of them paid to the several mortgagers assigns many of them according

And whereas the King's Majesty Commission of the Great Seal of Great Britain grounded upon several statutes made and now concerning bankruptcy 13th March 26th year of his present majesty was awarded against Thomas Abraham and directed to George Irton Esquire, Edmund Gibson and Hugh Holme gentlemen and also to William Milborne Esquire and John Park gentleman giving full power and authority to said commissioners named to start work and whereas John Lewthwaite and Peter Gale have been duly and legally chosen and appointed assignees the estate and effects of the said Thomas Abraham the bankrupt and whereas indenture of bargain and sale 9 February 1754 from George Irton, Edmund Gibson, Hugh Holmes, William Melbourne & John Park to John Lewthwaite and Peter Gale subject to the mortgage in trust for the creditors and John Lewthwaite and Peter Gale by virtue said Commision

abd said bargain and sale became entitled to the equity and redemption of the said Swarthmoor Hall messuages, watercornmills, lands, tenements, royalties and hereditaments in parish of Ulverston and Plumpton

Whereas by Indenture quinquapartite 18th 19th February 1754

1/ Sir William Wentworth Bt Bretton Hall Yorkshire

2/ John Lewthwaite and Peter Gale merchants Whitehaven and assignees in bankruptcy against Thomas Abraham

3/ Thomas Abraham

4? Peter Nicholson

5/ Alexander Hoskins of Wigton gentleman

Said Sir William Wentworth for consideration therein entered did by the direction of said John Lintwhite, Peter Gale and Thomas Abraham grant, bargain and sale to Peter Nicholson all those premises in the above partly recited indenture release tripartite 24th December 1743 particularly named excepting The Great Clott, the Little Clott Land & The Starr and Lund Meadows Barn Beck and the West End Close, The West End Meadow, two Windhill Meadows were to be be sold and conveyed by said Thomas Abraham before he became bankrupt by and with consent of Sir William Wentworth to John Dodgson of Ulverston- to hold the said premises for the uses hereinafter named that is to say to the use of Sir William Wentworth and his heirs and assigns for 500 years without impeachment of waste and after that to the use and behoof of Alexander Hoskins his heirs and assigns for ever, the said 500 years be void if Alexander Hoskins pay to Sir William Wentworth £3724-9-9 by 11th November next with interest but subject to the agreement only in one indenture of defeasance tripartite 19th February 1754 made or mentioned to be made between said Alexander Hoskins 1/, Peter Nicholson 2/, and said John Lewthwaite and Peter Gale 3/ hereinafter in part recited whereas the above named John Abraham sometime before the 19th conveyed equity of redemption of Swarthmoor Hall to his son Daniel Abraham {{ This is a mistake Daniel was John's father, The son was Thomas who

became bankrupt, however this document calls him Daniel several more times}} who afterwards became bankrupt and whereas the said Peter Nicholson sometime after the said Daniel Abraham became bankrupt purchased equity of redemption from assignees of commission of bankruptcy against said Daniel Abraham

Said Sir William Wentworth Bt and said Peter Nicholson by indenture of Lease and release 18th, 19th February 1754 which release was tripartite

1/ Sir William Wentworth Bart of Bretton Hall Yorks

2/ Peter Nicholson

3/ Alexander Hoskins

Alexander Hoskins alienates several messuages dwelling houses and premises situated in Manchester aforesaid which were conveyed by mortgage to Sir William Wentworth by John Abraham be transferred to Alexander Hoskins subject nonetheless to redemption by said Peter Nicholson. Alexander Hoskins does by consent and direction of John Lewthwaite and Peter Gale consent and agree that in pursuance of the several sums of money subject never the less (as to the premises in Ulverston and Plumpton Moss in parish of Ulverston to be redeemed by said John Lewthwaite and Peter Gale whereas said William Wentworth by indenture 11th November 1754

1/ Sir William Wentworth

2/ Alexander Hoskins

William Wentworth grants to Alexander Hoskins all the messuages, mills, lands tenements which were to be William Wentworths for 500 years by the above in part recited release 19th February 1754 except above next several closes passed to john Dodgeson. And whereas the Kings Majesty's Common Great Seal 18th December 1754 bankrupted said Peter Nicholson and directed Andrew Huddleston, William Milbourn,

George Irton esquires Edmund Gibson, Anthony Ponsonby gentlemen given full power and authority said commission four or three of them to execute the same and a majority of the commission began to act and whereas the said Matthias Gale one of the parties was the assignee of the commission for the estates and effects of the said Peter Nicholson the bankrupt. And whereas Anthony Ponsonby of the commission did find said Peter Nicholson was seized of the benefit and equity of remission of certain Messuages, mills, tenements, lands hereditaments in parish of Ulverston aforesaid then heretofore mortgage to him by said Thomas Abraham which he has assigned to said Matthias Gale and John Bell and Peter Nicholson above entitled to receive and benefit equity of remission of messuage or dwelling house in town of Manchester by him purchased from assignees of said Daniel Abraham the bankrupt conveyed to said Alexander Hoskins there mentioned and also to William Clough and his wife. And whereas by indenture 1 4 1755 between

1/ William Milbourn, George Irton & Anthony Ponsonby

2/ Matthias Gale

All those messuages in Manchester where Peter Nicholson has right and whereas some premises mortgaged by John Abraham to James Collins said James Collins by indenture 5th 6th January 1759

1/ James Collins gentleman Knaresbrough Yorks

2/ Henry Bainbridge gentleman Knaresbrough Yorks

Land on mortgage from John Abraham.

And whereas Matthias Gale and John Bell with consent and direction of Thomas Abraham and Peter Nicholson by indenture of lease and release 29th 30th January 1759

1/ Thomas Abraham & Peter Nicholson

2/ Matthias Gale & John Bell

3/ Anthony Ponsonby

Bargain and sale to use of Anthony Ponsonby all premises above recited

And whereas Matthias Gale and John Bell by Indenture Lease and Release 29th 30th January 1759

Conveyed to Anthony Ponsonby all those messuages mills lands tenements hereditaments in Ulverston in the land of Thomas Abraham and Peter Nicholson 8th 9th May 172x

And all those messuages dwelling houses premises in Manchester and parish of Manchester

Comprise indenture of John Abraham to William Wentworth 23rd 24th December 1743 and all benefits and equity of redemption that Matthia Gale had until Peter Nicholson had at time before bankruptcy to hoof and use of said Anthony Ponsonby

And whereas the several persons party to the presents have agreed to join in the absolute sale and conveyance of the messuage, mills lands tenements and premises (except the premises hereditaments botcchlrtn conveyed to John Dodgeson and Thomas Fisher as aforesaid) and to pay off and satisfy the several incumbrances affixed to such property as same will. And whereas after several weeks notice was given in the General Evening Post and other published news papers and the sale of the said premises the same when offered in public sale (subject to such mortgages made to the said William Clowes and Elizabeth Skelmerdine and also subject to the £600 settlement paid to the younger children of said John and Sarah Abraham at death of said John Abraham), to the above named Thomas Petty who was found to be the best bidder for such premises at the sum of £9675/16/-which was best price and most money. There now appears to be justly due to said Alexander Hoskins for principle about £6411/13/- And there now appears due to Henry Bainbridge £945/13/- And there now appears to be justly due to Anthony Ponsonby £2317/10/1 which with the four several sums of 5/- also due to (John Lewthwaite??) Peter Gale Thomas Abraham & Peter Nicholson made together the sum of £9675/16/-.

Now therefore this indenture witnesses that the sum of £6411/13/- to said Alexander Hoskins was paid by said Thomas Petty at request and direction of said John Lewthwaite, Peter Gale, Thomas Abraham, Anthony Ponsonby and Peter Nicholson.

And further the sum of £945/13./- was paid to Henry Bainbridge by Thomas Petty and further the sum of £2311/10/- was paid to Anthony Ponsonby by Thomas Petty

All acquit Thomas Petty of any further liability

All parties hear bargain and sale sold, assign and retail ratified to Thomas Petty Swarthmoor Hall and all barns, stables, outhouses and appurtenances. Levey Heads by esitimation 12 acres, Holm Field by estimation 6 roods, Curwen Estate with the barn by estimation 24 acres, Addison 's Field by estimation 15 acres, Little Widow meadow by estimation 6 roods Lower Little Widow by estimation 5 roods Great Widow Meadow by estimation3 acres 2 roods, Two Blundell Fields by estimation 5 acres 2 roods, Ellithorne Farm The Croft and High Field with additions 5 acres. Gale Croft 3acres 3 roods, Stale Close and Clow Petts 3 acres 2 roods. Round Levy Heads

5 acres, Harrison Close 2 acres, Little Levy heads 1acre 1 rood, Long Dales 3 acres, Great Dales 6 acres 2 roods, Little Greedy Ford 1 acre 2 roods, Round Levy Heads Brow, Long Dales Brow, and Greedy Ford Brow all planted with young wood 6 acres and Petty Gill and bank with the spring of yews on it 2 acres 2 roods, The Anglesea Close 2 acres 2 roods, Reginald Holme Close by estimation 3 acres, Dodgson wife Close 2 acres 2 roods, Kiln Close and the Gill and the wood growing there 2 acrs, Greedy Ford meadow, Old Wife Close, Stand Meadow Close, Roof Close and Dragley 18 acres Copy Close 4 acres Dicky Croft and Jackson's Dyke Meadow 6 acres Miller Holme and bank planted with oak wood 16 acres The Nicky at Spittlepotts Close 1 acre 2 roods The Holm 4 acrs 2 roods

High Bridge Meadow, Broad Dale and Bensons Meadow 10 acre and the house erected at the close called Croftlands 2 acres two other closes called the Lund Meadows 4 acres. Another close called the Great Coat lands 5 ½ acres

Sands Moss, High Moss, Round Potts Moss Becksike Moss, Old Causeway Moss, Round Potts Moss, Greystone Moss, Next Ness Moss, Raim Hill Moss

Three water corn mills called Over Mill, Town Mill and Ellers Mill and Kilns. One tenement called Scroggs at Over Mill

Moor Intack and Copeland Meadow Ulverston and Plumton Moss

Several messuages dwelling houses and interest of land of said John Abraham situated in Manchester and now in several occupations of Thomas Battersby, Robert Chapman, John Leigh, John Oldham and John Clough and others

[This last sheet mainly wrapping up minor details and I ran out of steam].

Signed and sealed by Peter Nicholson, Anthony Ponsonby, Henry Bainbridge, Alexander Hoskins, Ellen Abraham, Thomas Abraham, Peter Gale John Lewthwaite

Witnesses Elizabeth Gibson, P J Heywood

Receipts from Alexander Hoskins, Anthony Ponsonby and Henry Bainbridge

Document 16 14 February 1759 Indenture *at Friends House.*

1/ James Jackson hatter Ulverston

2/ John Lewthwaite and Peter Gale both merchants White haven (assignees of the commission wherein and under commission of bankruptcy awarded against Thomas Abraham late grocer Whitehaven) and Thomas Petty gentleman Ulverston

The redemption in the premises tenement most particularly mentioned late estate of John Abraham father Thomas Abraham and afterwards said Thomas Abraham vested by John Lewthwaite and Peter Gale in hands of said Thomas Petty for the purpose of granting a conveyance to the several real purchasers and whereas James Jackson having a grant for purchase subject to a charge of £600 settled upon the younger children of said John Abraham by virtue of a settlement made on the marriage of John Abraham and Sarah his wife and payable to said younger children on death of the said John Abraham and also subject to the payment of £25/16/- per annum as interest on £600 during life of said John Abraham to commence from this day hence

James Jackson takes on this charge and other expense of John Lewthwaite, Peter Gale & Thomas Petty

Capital messuage and various field as in document 15 will pay John Abraham the £25/16/- per annum and on his death the £600 to John Lewthwaite,, Peter Gale and Thomas Petty for the younger children of John Abraham

Witnesses Edward Garnett, Bryan Christopherson

Indenture four parts 1 6 1771

1/ Thomas Forster grocer City of Durham executor last will and testament Robert Forster gentleman Hawthorn deceased

2/ Robert Abraham merchant Nansendsound River Virginia, Ebenezer Miller late Manchester merchant and Margaret his wife, Otto Cook, John

Taylor, John Gatcliffe assignees under a commission of bankruptcy of the estates and effects said Ebenezer Miller, Thomas Hartley gentleman of Baildon and Rachel his wife, Robert Gray of Philadelphia Pennsylvania and Mary his wife, Alice Abraham and Hannah Abraham spinster Skerton near Lancaster

3/ William Lindow Esquire Lancaster

4/ John Rawlinson merchant Lancaster

Whereas by indenture of Lease and Release 16th 17th November 1722 tripartite

1/ Daniel Abraham and Rachel his wife of Swarthmoor Hall both since deceased and John Abraham his son and heir

2/ Thomas Forster of Hawthorn

3/ and Sarah Forster spinster daughter Robert Forster

Daniel Abraham and John Abraham by consideration of a marriage between John Abraham and Sarah Forster pass Swarthmoor Hall to Robert Forster

Viz:- Two Hind Meadows by estimation 4 acres, Starr Meadow by estimation 5 acres, Lund Cragg by estimation 1 acre, Kirby Meadow by estimation 1 acre, Whitwell Meadows by estimation 1 acre, Great Coat Lands by estimation 3 acres, Little Coat Lands by estimation 2 acres, The Style Close by estimation 3 acres, West End Meadow and West End Close by estimation 1 acre, Gale Croft by estimation 4 acres, Laith Close by estimation 2 acres the lye Corn thereon, Blendall Field by estimation 5 acres, Greater Widow Acres by estimation 5 acres, the two Lesser Widow Acres by estimation 2 acres, Addison Fields by estimation 15 acres, The Curwen's Estate by estimation 15 acres, Old Wife Howe and Lund by estimation 6 acres Longdales at Trinkeld by estimation 1 acre, Great Leavyheads by estimation 12 acres, Greedy Ford Meadows, Old Wife Close, Strange Close, Copy Ruff Close and Dragley by estimation 21 acres, Dicky Croft Land, The Holmes and Millom Hole by estimation 1acre, Gutterlands and the Tarn by estimation 1 acre, Low Bridge Meadow and Jackson's Dyke Meadow by estimation 3 acres, The two Bosseys by estimation 3 acres, Alletson Field by estimation 8 acres, Spittle Pott Ground, High Bridge Meadow and Broaddale by estimation 9 acres Round Leavy Heads by estimation 8 acres, Little Leavy Heads by estimation 2 roods, The Long Dales, The Great Dales, Little Greedy Ford Close by estimation 10 acres, Three water corn mills Over, Town and Ellers, Parcel of ground called The Scroggs adjacent to Over Mill by estimation 1 acre all in Ulverston in tenure Daniel & John Abraham

Waste, went green, paths, passages, easements, watercourses

All to use of Daniel Abraham and Rachel his wife for term of their natural lives and the longer lived of them and after their death to the use of the said John Abraham and his heirs and assigns until the said marriage took effect

{document recites list of lands for the children said John and Sarah Abraham} profits said premises for 400 years to Margaret, Rachel, Mary, Alice, Hannah and Robertr all of whom are 21

Premises came to Thomas Abraham who later became bankrupt

Premises sold to James Jackson felt maker Ulverston on behalf of James Jackson

£100 to be paid to Robert Abraham.

£100 to be paid to Thomas Otho, John Taylor, John Gatliffe at direction of Ebenezer Miller and Margaret his wife

£100 to be paid to Thomas Hartley and Rachel his wife

£100 to be paid to Robert Grey and Mary his wife

£100 to be paid to Alice Abraham

£100 to be paid to Hannah Abraham

APPENDIX G

THE APPEAL FOR HELP AFTER THE SOUTERGATE FIRE OF 1641

LA QSB/1/252/21

Petition of Myles Towers, Katherin Petty, William Postlethwaite, William Coward, John Birckbeck and John Addison ; losses by fire creation dates 1641

Those whose names are hereunder written do signify unto all those who this may.......... That upon thirteenth day of July last about one of the afternoon, the house of Myles Towers of Soutergate in Ulverston was suddenly and casually set on fire, no body being then in the said house but the said Towers being a very old decrepit man, the fire whereon by reason of a violent and extreme west wynd did take hold of the houses being opposite thereunto, in the same street, and in a very short time consuming burned down eleven houses, whereof five were dwelling houses and the rest farms and workhouses. All of them consisting of 29 bays of building besides other houses nearer adjoining that were much ruined by the said fire, the charge of rebuilding the same in such sort as they were before as is...... ed by workmen will amount to near as 200L besides the losses sustained in their good consumed by the said fire amounting nearer upon 100L. The owners of the said houses being all of them very poor and altogether unabe to.... The said houses without the charitable relief of others, one of them being a poor widow hath five children, and the rest being very poor tradesmen and labourers

(Signed) Roger Kirkbye

(the 45 signatures include) Thomas Corker, Matthew Millerson, Roland Gawnson, William Gawnson, Robert Garnet, Richard Holme, John Holme, William Fell, Thomas Fell, John Dodgson, Roger Kirkbye, James Dolling, Thomas Fell, John Sawrey, Philip Bennett, ... Corker, Christofer Fell, Edward Geldard, John Monnf...., William Sawrey, Thomas Ashburner, Sawrey Jenkinson, Thomas Fell

William,,, William,,, William,,, Edward,,,, James,,,, William,,, William,,, Thomas,,,,

APPENDIX H

MAP OF JAMES LINDOW'S PROPOSED PURCHASES

Friends House MS Volume 364

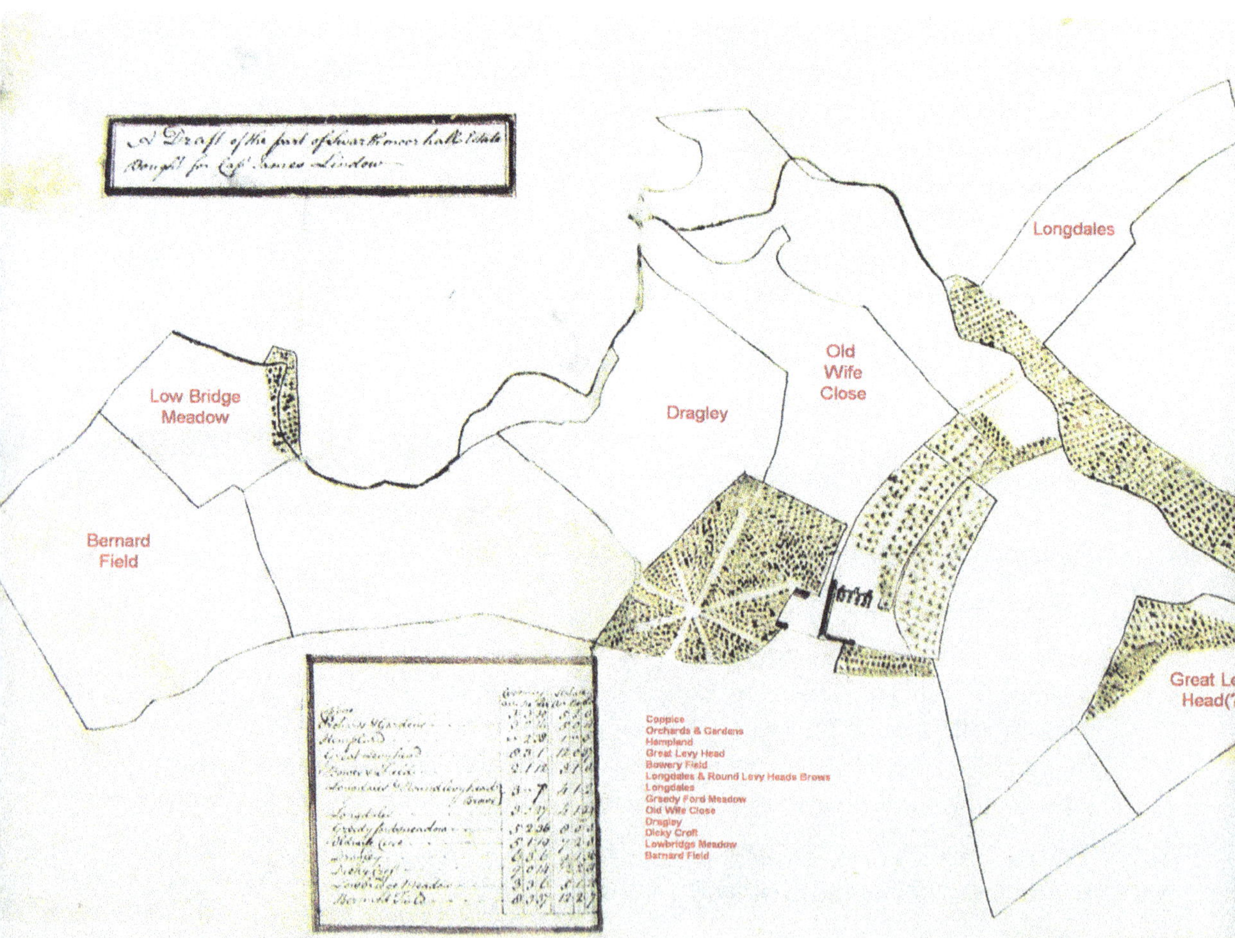

APPENDIX I

NOTES ON WILL OF WILLIAM LINDOW

LA WRW/A

Will of William Lindow merchant Lancaster 1787

trustees John Bowes esquire Lancaster, James Lucas esquire Hutton near Preston and Jackson Mason gentleman of Lancaster

land in Great Britain and Goyave Plantation in Grenada and Fountaine and Barrowallee Plantations in St Vincent

Bank End in Ulverston parish to use of trustees during life of my sister Ellinor wife of Mr James Jackson of Ulverston, income to be paid into her hand. After death said sister Ellinor and her husband their daughter Ann Jackson my niece to have Bank End absolutely

Arrad Foot to use of trustees during life of my brother in law Bryan Christopherson widower of my deceased sister Agnes. He having the income and after his death Arrad Foot to go to their daughter Elizabeth

Swarthmoor Hall to use of trustees during life of my niece Ann Jackson she to have the income and after her death to her sons in order and then her daughters in order

Topping Raise and Oxenhouse in Ulverston parish to use of trustees during life of Elizabeth Christopherson who is to have income and her children inherit after her death

Rent from West Indies to pay £50 per annum to sister Ellinor to cover bond to Thomas Petty for £30 per annum to sister Ellinor

Residue to wife Abigail who is executor with trustees, then failing heirs of his body to any son or daughter of Henry Rawlinson.

Henry Lindow Rawlinson son said Henry Rawlinson to inherit estate in St Vincent and take name Lindow

Abraham Tysack Rawlinson another son said Henry Rawlinson

Requests name and arms of Lindow be used by inheritors in female line

land in Tobago, two lots of land in St George Town Grenada and two lots of land in Prince Ruperts Bay Domenica. Goyave in Grenada, Fountains and Barrowallee in St Vincent

brother in law Thomas Rawlinson

bequests of £50 each to trustee and Thomas Petty of Ulverston, William Hull of Kendal and John Jackson of Lancaster my late clerk, Mr William Burnthwaite of Ulverston

Interest on £2000 to niece Ann Jackson

APPENDIX J

NOTES ON WILL OF ABIGAIL LINDOW WIDOW LANCASTER 1791

LA WRW/A

under 1780 will of my late father Abraham Rawlinson I inheritred Abbots Close and Haverbreck in Lancaster. These with premises at Lancaster and Burrow and £1000 to Abraham Tysack Rawlinson son of my brother Henry Rawlinson

Jane widow of brother John Rawlinson merchant Lancaster £1000

Ann wife of William Dickinson surgeon Broughton-in-Furness £500

Elizabeth wife Robert Carr of Liverpool and daughter of Bryan Christopherson £500

Samuel Gawitts gentleman Ulverston £100, his wife Elizabeth £100

Jackson Mason gent to have £50, servant Hannah Faulkner to have £200

executors brothers William Rawlinson, Thomas Rawlinson and Samuel Rawlinson and Jackson Mason

interest on £1000 to niece Marion eldest daughter brother Henry Rawlinson and wife of Robert Hesketh esquire.

other daughters of brother Henry, Ellen wife of Revd Gilbert Ainslie and Elizabeth Rawlinson and Martha Rawlinson

APPENDIX K

TERTIARY EDUCATION OF LOW FURNESS GENTRY

The information is derived from Joseph Foster's "Admissions to Gray's Inn 1521-1889" and his "Alumni Oxoniensis 1500-1714" and Venn's "Alumni Cantabrigensis" together with information supplied by the archivist of University College Oxford. Foster used the University's register of admissions. The College kept its own.

George Dodding - admitted fellow commoner Emanuel Cambridge 4 7 1623 son and heir Miles Dodding of Conishead matriculated 1623

Admitted to Grays Inn 15 8 1628 when of Conishead

Married Sarah daughter Rowland Backhouse and died ca 1651

George Dodding admitted Gray's Inn 15 8 1628 son and heir Miles Dodding of Conishead Esquire

Miles Dodding matriculated St John Cambridge 1557/8

Miles Dodding son of George Dodding above admitted fellow commoner of St John's Cambridge 23 May 1659 aged 17 matriculate 1659

a JP

Married Margaret daughter Roger Kirkby of Kirkby will 1683

Thomas Fell of County of Lancaster gentleman matriculated University College Oxford 23 6 1621 aged 19 BA 29 5 1623

Thomas Fell admitted Gray's Inn 20 10 1623 son and heir George Fell of Ulverston County of Lancaster gentleman

George Fell admitted fellow commoner at Christ's College Cambridge 6 7 1655 aged 15 son of Thomas Fell the judge of Swarthmoor Hall

School Little Urswick under Mr Ingman

Admitted Gray's Inn 9 2 1656/7 son of Thomas Fell of Swarthmore + 1670

George Fell admitted Grays Inn 9 2 1652/3 eldest son Thomas Fell of Swarthmoor County of Lancaster esquire

George Fell son and heir Thomas Fell esquire one of the benchers of the society 16 7 1655

John Fell of Gray's Inn gentleman admitted Gray's Inn 11 10 1749

William Scandrell Fell pruvines 'tonsor' 7 10 1794

Robert Fell 'tonsor' pruvinese 27 11 1802 Oxford

John Kirkby admitted pensioner to St John's College Cambridge aged 15 on 24 5 1631 son of Roger Kirkby of Kirkby Ireleth

School Sedbergh admitted Lincoln's Inn 3 3 1639/40 + 1680

Richard Kirkby admitted fellow commoner Caius College Cambridge 5 7 1575 son of Roger Kirkby of Kirkby Ireleth

Admitted Gray's Inn from Barsage in 30 January 1576/7

Richard Kirkby admitted Gray's Inn 13 6 1640 son and heir Roger Kirkby of Kirkby Ireleth County Lancaster esquire

Curwen Rawlinson matriculated Queen's College Oxford 10 3 1656/7 son of Robert Rawlinson of Cark in Cartmel incumbant 9 2 1671/2

Married Elizabeth Monk (2nd daughter and coheir Nicholas Monk Bishop of Herefotd and niece of General Monk Duke of Albemarle) MP for Lancaster 1689 + August 1689

Christopher Rawlinson admiited as pensioner to Magdalene College Cambridge 14 6 1694 aged 17 son of Curwen Rawlinson

Matriculated Queen's College Oxford 14 6 1695 aged 18 son of Curwen Rawlinson

Of Kirk Hale + Holborn Bar Row Lincolns Inn + 8 1 1732/3

Monk Rawlinson admitted fellow commoner of Magdalen College Cambridge 28 5 1691 aged 17 son of Curwen Rawl;inson, vicar of Garstang 14 July 1692 + 1692

Thomas Rawlinson pleb County Lancaster matriculated 2 11 1621 aged 18 at Brasenose College Oxford BA 1 2 1626/7

Matthew Richardson of County of Lancaster pleb matriculated Queen's Col;ege Oxford 26 10 1599 aged 16

Matthew Richardson son of Matthew Richardson of Ravenheads County Lancaster matriculated Queens College Oxford 9 11 1632 aged 17

Matthew Richardson admitted Gray's Inn 2 2 1637/8 son and heir Matthew Richardson of Ravenheads County Lancaster

Thomas Richardson admitted Gray's Inn 30 7 1663 son and heir Matthew Richardson of Rownehead County Lancaster esquire

William Corker pleb matriculated Brasenose College Oxford 30 10 1635 aged 16 son of Francis Corker of Ulverston. Fellow BNC 1648

Christopher Preston matriculated Queen's College Oxford 4 12 1618 aged 17 son of George Preston of Holker BA 26 6 1622

Thomas Preston matriculated Queen's College Oxford 30 % 1627 aged 17 son of George Preston of Holker. MP for Lancaster 1665-1678

George Preston matriculated Brasenose College Oxford 21 6 1662 aged 16 son of Thomas Preston of Holker above

Gilbert Preston matriculate Queen's College Oxford 28 1 1667 aged 17 son of Thomas Preston of Cartmel

Richard Lower gentleman matriculated Christ Church College Oxford 27 2 1650/1 student 1649, Bmed and D Med 28 6 1668 FRS

Son of Humphrey Lower of Tremere Cornwall baptised St Tudy 29 1 1631

+ 17 1 1690/1 buried St Tudy

There seems to be a pattern of Furness entry going to University and then afterwards going on to Gray's Inn. That being so it makes it more likely that the Thomas Fell who attendeed University College Oxford son of a Lancashire gentleman was in fact Judge Fell

ABBREVIATIONS

BHO British History on Line

BRO Cumbria County Archives Barrow Record Office

CJ Journal of the House of Commons

CL Journal of the House of Lords

CSPD Calendar of State Papers Domestic

CW Cumberland and Westmorland Antiquarian and Archaeological Society Journal

FH Friends House

KRO Cumbria County Archives Kendal Record Office

LA Lancashire Archives Preston

NA National Archives Kew

BIBLIOGRAPHY

L R Ayre - *Guide to Ulverston*

Henry Birkett -*The Story of Ulverston*

A P Bridson -*Two Lakeland Parishes*

British History Online

William Caton - *Autobiography*

A Craven -*The Commonwealth of England and The Govenors of Lancashire New Modelised and Cromwellised* Northern History 48 (1) pages 41-58

Joseph Foster -*Pedigrees of County Families - Lancaster, Alumni Oxoniensis, Register of Gray's Inn*

George Fox -*Journal*

Margaret Fell - *A Relation* publsshe J Sowle 1710

William Fell - *History and Antiquities of Furness*

E B Fryde, D. Greenwood, S Porter & L Roy -*Handbook of British Chronolgy*

J M Gratton -*The Parliamentary and Royalist War Effort in Lancashire*

Richard Hoyle -*Tudor Taxation Records*

Jonathan Huddlestone -*The children's teeth are set on edge*

Matthew Keegan - *Ashlack*

S Lewis -*Topological dictionary of England*

Mary Mason - *Childhood Days at Swarthmoor Hall - Growing up in a Quaker Manor House*

Thomas Mouncey - *An account of the life of Thomas Fell*

Anne C Parkinson - *A History of Catholicism in the Furness Peninsula 1127-1997*

George Omerod - *Remains Historical and Literary connected with the Palatine Counties* Chetham Society Vol II.

Isabel Ross - *Margaret Fell - Mother of Quakerism*

Robert Somerville -*Office-Holders in the Duchy and County Palatine of Lancaster from 1603*

Maria Webb -*The Fells of Swarthmore Hall*

Thomas West -*Antiquities of Furness*

Peter Wilde -*Ulverstone, Life in Georgian Ulverston 1720-1830*

William Retlaw Williams -*The history of the Great Session in Wales 1542-1830*

Blair Worden -*The Rump Parliament* and *The English Civil Wars*

David Underwood -*Prides Purge*

REFERENCES BY CHAPTER

Chapter 1 - The Name Swarthmoor

1. A P Brydson "Two Lakeland Parishes - Blawith and Nibthwaite quoting inquisition post mortem of John de Coupland 1358
2. 30Henry VIII 1538-9 Record Society of Lancashire and Cheshire xxxv page 100-104
3. National Archives E179/130/162
4. Homberstsons survey 1569 NA Exchequor King's Remembrancer Misc Books Vol 38/17-22
5. Lancashire Fines 11-20 Edward III Final concords for Lancashire, Part 2, 1307-77 (1902)
6. Volume 12 Record Society of Lancashire and Cheshire (Miscellanies Volume 1) page 220 Citing Book of Composition for refusing knighthoods at King Charles's coronation which provides information in square brackets And Exchequor Records Exchequor QR special Commission No 5389.

Chapter 2 - The Fells

7. NA Exchequer King's Rembrancer Misc Books Vol 38/17-22 in CW 2nd series volume 29 pages 339-400 known as Homberston's Survey Actually a survey of the whole of Sir John Neville's Estate by Edmund Hall and William HOMBERSTON
8. BRO BDX 628 17th Century
9. BRO BDX 209/2/21/1 conveyance moss at Beckar Sykes 30 6 1612
10. BRO BDHJ 2/2/1 feoffment of 23 March 1613 11James I
11. BRO BDX 209/2/21/2 deed of 30 4 1618
    11a BRO BDS 19/T1 Feoffment Ulverston Town Bank School Deeds 26 November 1607
12. Volume 12 Record Society of Lancashire and Cheshire (Miscellanies Volume 1) page 220 Citing Book of Composition for refusing knighthoods at King Charles's coronation which provides information in square brackets And Exchequor Records Exchequor QR special Commission No 5389
13. Joseph Forster "Alumni Oxonensis " also matriculation register of the University of Oxford and regarding his financial position in University College information from the archivist of that college

14. Joseph Foster "Alumni Gray's Inn'

15. Maria Webb "The Fells of Swarthmoor Hall page 120/121

16. KRO WD RAD/T 18 feoffment of 3 1 1649 reciting feoffment of 19 9 1634

17. KRO WD RAD/T 18 feoffment of 3 1 1649

18. Henry Forrest Birkett " The Story of Ulverston" By direction of parliament he was placed on the Commission of the Peace for Lancashire in 1641 However The House of Lords appointed a Commission of the Peace for Lancashire including Thomas Fell 24th October 1642 Volume 5 Journal House of Lords BHO, BHO also reports a commision to raise £4353/11/3 from Lancashire in 1640 and Thomas Fell was on that as well

19. Appendix G being a copy of a transcript of LA QSB/1/252/21 made by Mrs Elizabeth Ellis - the original can no longer be produced at LA

20. Maria Webb "The Fells of Swarthmoor Hall pp356-360

21. Record Society Lancashire & Cheshire - Volumes 24 26 29 36 72 95 & 96 Royalist Composition Papers

22. Ordinances of the Commonwealth Ritt and Firth

23. "Return of the Name of Every member of the Lower House of Parliament of England, Scotland, And Ireland, with Name of Constiuency Represented and Date of Return, From 1213-1874" printed by order of the House of Commons 1 March 1878

24. (SP19-118 no 53 reported in The Rump Parliament by Blair Worden)

25. Journal House of Commons

26. David Underdown "Prides Purge" and see "Remains Historical and literary connected with the Palatine Counties"

27. Blair Worden "The Rump Parliament"

28. Journal House of Commons and A Craven "The Commonwealth of England and the Governors of Lancashire - New Modelised and Cromwelised" Northern History 48 (1) pp 41-58

29. "Return of the Name of every member of the lower House of Parliament of England Scotland and Ireland with name of every constituency represented and date of return from 1213 to 1874" published by House of Commons 1878

30. CJ 15 9 1646 pages 668-670 County of Lancashire divided into nine classical presbyteries and Nicholas Clarke, George Dodding Esquires Thomas Fell, Edward Rigby, Adam Sandes of Booth, John Sawrey of Plumpton, William xxxxx, Robert Rawlinson of Greenhead gentlemen, Thomas Fell of Scarthwaite gentleman, Thomas Danson of Lxxx, Richard Myres of Beckxxxx, William Rawlinson of Greythwaite gent were appointed to Classis No 9

31. Cheshire Archives ZA /B/2/79v-80 20 11 1646

32. City of Chester Assembly, Assembly Books Second Assembly Book.
Thomas Fell barrister at law elected learned counsel of the City in place of John Ratcliffe and ZA/B/2/101v 4th Feb 1652/3
John Santhey, esquire, an utter barrister at law, elected City Counsel in place of Thomas

Fell, esquire who had becme one of the Chief Justices of the County of Chester. Also 6th March 1647 index CJ ordinance appointing Thomas Fell and Humphrey Mackworth attorneys general of North Wales agreed by Lords March 6th LJ And Ordered that Mr Fell be 2nd Judge of Chester in room of Mr Justice Warburton and the Lords Commissioners of the Great Seal of England be authorised and required to pais and patent of the Great Seal of England unto the said Mr Fell accordingly -CJ

33. Reference from Duchy of Lancaster Rental and Surveys at NA by A P Brydson in "Two Lakeland Parishes - Blawith & Nibthwaite"
34. "Office-holders in the Duchy and Country Palatine of Lancaster from 1603" Robert Somerville
35. Acts and Ordinances Vol 1 pages 92,114,149,546,707,758,968,1086 & 1239 Volume 2 pages 301,469,666,750,972 & 1072
36. Memoria by Bulstrode Whitelock MP 11 October 1658 Mr Fell died, he was a good lawyer and a good man, he served the parliament as a soldier and they made him commissioner of the seal for Lancashire and second judge of Chester.He also reports Fell being made Chancellor of the Duchy of Lancaster and a Judge in Chester and North Wales
37. David Underdown "Prides Purge"
38. Liverpool Town Book Lancashire and Cheshire Record Society Volume 136 for 1999 pages 2 and 51
39. Article on Force Forge by Brian G Awty in CWAAS volume 77 for 1977 pp97-112
40. KRO WD RAD/T 18 feoffment of 3 January 1649
41. KRO WD RAD/T 19 Bargain & Sale 19 September 1650, Endorsement enrolled in Chancery 31 December 1650
42. BRO Bdx 628 Receipt 2 2 1670. Also Furness Compert Book for 1685 where she is listed as not paying assessment and called Dame Hannah Fell
43. CSPD Charles 2 entry volume iv/21 Doc Ref SP 29/4 f21
44. CSPD SP44/16 f 311 dated 4 1 1664/5 Volume cx (24c). And CSPD SP29/110 folio 31 page no 161 January 1664/5
45. Isabel Ross "Margaret Fell the mother of Quakerism" Pages 220 et seq.
46. CSPD 1671 Vol 25 NO 38 Docquets 171 ex 1329 4 April 1671 according to Bonnelyn Young Kuntzel
47. Acts and Ordinances page 1371
48. CJ 18 August 1651 & 17 September 1651 and preface to volume 1 part 1 of "Catalogue of the Pamphlets, Books, Newspapers and Manuscripts Relating to the Civil War, the Commonwealth and the Restoration, collected by George Thomason 1640-1661" by G K Fortescue and others
49. Isabel Ross reporting paper in possession of Lord Wakefield page 324
50. KRO WD RAD/T20 articles of agreement 6 6 1691

Excursus I: The Date The Hall Was Built

51. "Journal of the Life and Religious labours of Thomas Scattergood Minister of the Gospel of the Society of Friends" Philadelphia Friends Book Store pages 284-285
52. S Lewis "Topological Dictionary of England
53. L R Ayre "Guide to Ulverston and Places of Interest in Lake Land" Ulverston 1904
54. "Conservation Report" by Architectural History Practice for Britain Yearly Meeting September 2017 - Marion Baxter, Dan Ellsworth & Robert Harrington
55. History & Antiquities of Furness By William Fell S B aged 11 years. Printed from original manuscript and edited by L R Ayre MA vicar Holy Trinity Ulverston 1887- Volume 1
56. Appendix H FH MS Volume 364

Excursus II: The Other Fells

57. This will and others unless otherwise specified are at Lancashire Record Office Preston WRW F with name of testator and date
58. BRO BDHJ 49/10/1 Deed 13 April 1737
59. "Ulverstone Life in Georgian Ulverston 1720-1830" Peter Wilde page 5 illustrated by modern photograph of hopperhead on James Fell's house inscribed I F 1736
60. BRO BDX 209/2/21/5 and BRO BDFELL/4/15 Lease 12 1 1668 and History of the family of Fell of Dalton Gate
61. LA QSJ -5-8-24 Sacrament Certificates Bundle 8

Excursus III: The Servants

62. Much of this excursus relies on Isabel Ross "Margaret Fell" and Maria Webb "The Fells of Swarthmoor Hall"
63. BRO BSUDU/c/Box/3/1/4
64. Placeholder
65. Autobiography of William Caton

Excursus IV: Margaret Fell's Background

66. KRO WD RAD/T 18 feoffment 3 1 1649
67. LA WRWF estate of Matthew Richardson
68. KRO WD RAD/T 18 feoffment 3 1 1649
69. The will of Richard Askew of Marsh Grange 1551 is in a set of deeds at Barrow Record Office. All the other wills are at Lancashire Record Office Preston reference WRW /F
70. J Brownbill in CW 2nd series number 10 pages 331-341
71. J Brownbill in CW 2nd series number 10 pages 331-341
72. Acts and Ordinances pages 890 and 891

Chapter Three: The Abrahams

73. "Pedigrees of the County Families of England" by Joseph Foster Volume 1 Lancashire 1873
74. The sale of Hauxwell in 1697 is often asserted. I have not so far found a contemporary reference or deed of sale. Another family is of Hauxwell later on
75. NA E/134/1Anne?Mich12 8th March 1702 to 9th March 1707
76. Isabel Ross "Margaret Fell mother of Quakerism" p339
77. Isabel Ross "Margaret Fell mother of Quakerism page 363 quoting page 226-7 of H.G Crosfield's transcript of Abraham Mss 37 of 22 November 1697-8
78. BRO BDHJ 446 1 3 Conveyance 9 11 1726
79. BRO BDHJ /1/T44 sale 17 1 1723
80. "Two Lakeland Parishes" (Blawith and Nibthwaite) by A P Brydson
81. BRO BDX 209/1/36/7 deed of 29 July 1729 and BDX 209/1/36/8 deed of 30th January 1729
82. BRO BDX 209/1/36/9 mortgage 2 February 1730
83. BRO BDX 628 15th August 1700 6th August 1702
84. West "Antiquities of Furness" followed by Isabel Ross
85. BRO BDHJ 2/2/1 Feoffment 23 3 1613 11James 1
86. "Ashlack the history of a small Cumbrian estate" by Mark Keegan
87. Appendix F referring to Thomas Petty's resolution of Thomas Abraham's financial affairs & FH document 16 of 14 2 1759 referring to lease and release of 16th 17th November 1722
88. Appendix F 11th&12th February 1746
89. Joseph Foster "Pedigree of Foster of Hawthorn Co Durham"
90. Isabel Ross page and Quaker burial register
91. Note by Harper Gaythorp in J Brownbill CW 2nd series number 10 pages 331-341
92. BRO BDS 26/8 letter 13 9 1845
93. BRO BDX 209/1/36 Indenture 1 2 1728
94. BRO BDKF 261/2/14/6 conveyance 7 1 1736
95. BRO BDKF 261/2/14/5 indenture February 1727
96. BRO BDX 209/136/8 mortgage and release 30 January 1729
97. BRO BDX 209/1/36/25&26 Petty Richardson Deeds 1740
98. BRO BDX 209/1/36/6 Indenture 1 2 1728
99. LA DDBB 4-4 receipt of manorial due 6 November 1731
100. BRO BDX 209/1/36 Petty Richardson 31 January 1737
101. BRO BDX 209/1/36/9 deed 1736 & BDX 209/1/36/14 Petty Richardson deed
102. BRO BDX 209/1/36/23&24 1739 Petty-Richardson

103. BRO BDHJ 108/16/1 5th&6th June 1736

104. A P Bridson "Two Lakeland Parishes" deed 29 10 1736

105. BRO BDHJ 49/10/1 Deed 134 4 1737

106. FH Indenture of Lease and Release 23rd 24th July 1735 & referred to in BRO BDHJ 108/16/1

107. FH Mortgage 24th December 1743 & referred to in BRO BDHJ 108/16/1

108. BRO BDHJ 108/16/1 Lease and Release 10 11 1747

109. BRO BDX 209/2/21/12 deed of 18 12 1740

110. Manchester University Library Rylands Papers RYCH 660 dated 1743

111. Appendix F 5th&6th January 1759

112. Appendix F 24 December 1743

113. BRO Z140 lease 8 5 1752 & Z143 Lease and Release 8&9 5 1752

114. Father of Jane Gale who married Wilson Gale Braddyll of Conishead Priory who was his cousin's son. Matthias was nephew to the George Gale who was second husband of President Washington's grandmother. Peter Gale who also features in the financial affairs of Thomas Abraham was a second cousin

115. BRO BD /143/1 Lease & Release 12th & 13th June 1752

116. Appendix F & BRO Z/143/1 Memorandum 10th February 1753

117. Appendix F 29th&30th January 1759 & BRO Z/143/1 30 January 1759

118. BRO BDX 209/2/36/2 indemnity bond 1759

119. BRO BDX 209/2/36/1 indemnity bond 1759

120. Appendix F 18th 19th February 1754 & BRO BDHJ Presendent Book 2 pages 77-78

121. Article by Ian Lewis in "Swarthmoor Hall Historian Volume 1 no 1" citing Burney Collection of 17th and 18th century newspapers and specifically the London Evening Post; issue 3456 23rd-26th December 1749, issue 3779 7th-9th January 1752 issue 3966 27th-29th March 1753 and issue 4188 14th-17th September 1754 & London Gazette issue 9207 12th-15th May 1753, issue 9501 9th-12th August 1755 and issue 9484 10th-14th June 1755

122. Seven part indenture of 1759 by Thomas Petty Appendix F

123. NA E 134/4GeoIII/East9 Interogatories, Deposition taken at Ulverston 2 April 4 Geo III 1764 John Abraham & his wife Sarah paupers v. Alexander Hoskins, John Collins, Edmund Gibson, John Lewthwaite, Peter Nicholson, Pater Gale, Matthias Gale, Thomas Abraham, Zachery Hubbersty defendants. Concerning a capital mansion House called Swarthmoor Hall lately estate of the plaintiff John Abraham - Conveyance of the premises by the plaintiff to his son the defendant Thomas Abraham. Swarthmoor Hall Historian Volume 1 page 9

Chapter Four: The Lindows

124. LA WRWF name date and residence for all Lindow wills unless otherwise specified
125. Appendix H FH MS Volume 364
126. See Excursus 7
127. "The children's teeth are set on edge" Jonathan Huddleston 2010
128. Journal Board of Trade September 1765 folio 232 appointment of Wm Lindow, Acts Privy Council 1770 volume 174, page 296, Scotch, " The Caribbean and the Atlantic World" by Douglas Hamilton
129. BRO BDX 209/2/22.3 agreement 1 April 1754
130. BRO BPR 2/O/17/26 apprenticeship 16 May 1764
131. "The Rolls of the Freemen of the Borough of Lancaster 1688-1840" Pat 1 Lancashire & Cheshire Record Society volume LXXXVII (1935) page 195 cited in Centre for North West Regional Studies Regional Bulletin New Series No 13 Summer 1999
132. BRO BSUDU/L/20/1 Article of Agreement 3 6 1763
133. BRO Z 519 Bargain and Sale 2 1 1772
134. BRO BSUDU/C/21/29 Lease and Release 1766
135. BRO BDHJ 404/1/46 Chancery Ct Lancaster 10 George IV reciting Release Indenture 14 2 1783
136. BRO BDHJ 93/6 agreement of 4 March 1771
137. BRO BDHJ 404/1/47 Release of dower 22 2 1787
138. BRO ZS 531 1808 advertisement flier printed by John Soulby printer King St Ulverston,
139. BRO BDHJ declaration 23 July 1842 & FH MS Box 1/11 letter in which facts are stated accurately
140. Mrs Fletcher's willingness to pay money to school under Judge Fell's will reference found and lost.

Excursus VIII: The Tenants

141. All baptisms burials and weddings at Ulverston Parish Church and wills at Lancashire Record Office
142. London Gazette (London England) June 10-June 14th 1755 Issue 9484 via Burney Collection and Volume 1 Number 1 Swarthmoor Hall Historian
143. BRO BPR 2/0/13/37 apprenticeship by church wardens 14 6 1769
144. BRO BDX 209/2/14/1 indenture 18th century
145. BRO BDHJ 46/1 1765-95 Account Books
146. T G Holt article on Fr Thomas West in CWAA 2nd series volume 79
147. J Brownbill in CW 2nd series number 10 pages 331-341
148. BRO BSUDU/C/Box/3/¼ enclosure Act Deed 14 10 1838
149. BRO BSUDU/L/21/100 Lease 8 10 1847

150. BRO BDS 26/8 Letter 13 9 1845

151. BRO BDHJ 220/3/7 declaratio 23 7 1842

152. Swarthmoor Hall Historian Volume 4 article by Ian Lewis siting Soulby's Ulverston Advertiser 10th August 1854

153. Swarthmoor Hall Historian Volume 4 article by Ian Lewis siting Soulby's Ulverston Advertiser 9th Ocotober 1856

154. BRO BDHJ 20/3/9 Notice to quit 6 August 1857

155. BRO BDHJ 222/4/17 letter 8 10 1857

156. Swarthmoor Hall Historian volume 4 Summer 2014 citing Soulby May 6 1858

157. Sale particulars of Swarthmoor Hall.

158. "The Purchase of Swarthmoor Hall" Bulletin of Friends Historical Society of Philadelphia Volume 5 No 1 pages 20-22 April 1913

www.ingramcontent.com/pod-product-compliance
Ingram Content Group UK Ltd.
Pitfield, Milton Keynes, MK11 3LW, UK
UKHW050137280726
14058UKWH00006B/692